Cambridge Elements ≡

Elements in World Englishes
edited by
Edgar W. Schneider
University of Regensburg

INDIAN ENGLISHES IN THE TWENTY-FIRST CENTURY

Unity and Diversity in Lexicon and Morphosyntax

Sven Leuckert
Technische Universität Dresden

Claudia Lange
Technische Universität Dresden

Tobias Bernaisch
Justus Liebig University Giessen

Asya Yurchenko
Chemnitz University of Technology

CAMBRIDGE
UNIVERSITY PRESS

Shaftesbury Road, Cambridge CB2 8EA, United Kingdom

One Liberty Plaza, 20th Floor, New York, NY 10006, USA

477 Williamstown Road, Port Melbourne, VIC 3207, Australia

314–321, 3rd Floor, Plot 3, Splendor Forum, Jasola District Centre, New Delhi – 110025, India

103 Penang Road, #05–06/07, Visioncrest Commercial, Singapore 238467

Cambridge University Press is part of Cambridge University Press & Assessment, a department of the University of Cambridge.

We share the University's mission to contribute to society through the pursuit of education, learning and research at the highest international levels of excellence.

www.cambridge.org
Information on this title: www.cambridge.org/9781009454186

DOI: 10.1017/9781009323796

First published 2023

A catalogue record for this publication is available from the British Library

ISBN 978-1-009-45418-6 Hardback
ISBN 978-1-009-32378-9 Paperback
ISSN 2633-3309 (online)
ISSN 2633-3295 (print)

Indian Englishes in the Twenty-First Century

Unity and Diversity in Lexicon and Morphosyntax

Elements in World Englishes

DOI: 10.1017/9781009323796
First published online: November 2023

Sven Leuckert
Technische Universität Dresden

Claudia Lange
Technische Universität Dresden

Tobias Bernaisch
Justus Liebig University Giessen

Asya Yurchenko
Chemnitz University of Technology

Author for correspondence: Sven Leuckert, sven.leuckert@tu-dresden.de

Abstract: English fulfils important intra- and international functions in twenty-first-century India. However, the country's size in terms of area, population, and linguistic diversity means that completely uniform developments in Indian English (IndE) are unlikely. Using sophisticated corpus-linguistic and statistical methods, this Element explores the unity and diversity of IndE by providing studies of selected lexical and morphosyntactic features that characterise Indian English(es) in the twenty-first century. The findings indicate a degree of incipient 'supralocalisation', that is, a spread of features beyond their place of origin, cutting through the typological Indo-Aryan versus Dravidian divide.

Keywords: corpus linguistics, Indian Englishes, lexis, morphosyntax, World Englishes

ISBNs: 9781009454186 (HB), 9781009323789 (PB), 9781009323796 (OC)
ISSNs: 2633-3309 (online), 2633-3295 (print)

Contents

1 Introduction

The linguistic ecology of India, both past and present, and the position of English within it have never ceased to attract researchers from a wide range of fields, including historical linguistics, language contact, applied linguistics and English Language Teaching (ELT), sociology of language, and, last but not least, the study of postcolonial varieties of English (PCEs). Among world Englishes, Indian English (IndE) represents both the oldest and the largest second-language variety of English, with currently around 300 million speakers in India (Sridhar 2020: 245) and millions more in the diaspora. Indian institutions of higher education cater to the needs of many neighbouring states by offering degrees, teacher training, and refresher courses in/for English to their citizens. IndE thus far extends its original boundaries and may even be the regional epicentre (for a general discussion of the concept see Peters and Bernaisch 2022). The prominence of IndE is reflected in a large number of studies; it was squarely placed on the scholarly agenda by the late Braj Kachru's pioneering work (e.g. Kachru 1994). With the arrival of corpus linguistics and particularly with the ongoing *International Corpus of English* (ICE) project, most studies on IndE are now corpus-based, and this Element is no exception. It follows Wiltshire (2020) in focussing on the unity and diversity of contemporary IndE, complementing her phonological study with our emphasis on morphosyntax and the lexicon. However, our approach to IndE goes beyond other corpus-based studies, facilitated by our database (see Section 3): this Element is based on a contemporary set of semi-automatically generated, web-derived newspaper corpora of IndE, namely the *Corpus of Regional Indian Newspaper Englishes* (CORINNE; Yurchenko et al. 2021a, 2021b) and the Indian components of the 2020 update of the *South Asian Varieties of English Corpus* (SAVE2020; Bernaisch et al. 2021), representing acrolectal, supra-regional IndE. Since IndE is not yet codified, we adopt the assumption that the language use of English newspapers with a nationwide circulation is the best candidate or model for an emerging standard IndE (see Schilk 2011: 47). The newspaper language captured by CORINNE, on the other hand, is likely to reflect more regional usage, which in turn may be determined by different factors, among them regionally specific language contact scenarios as well as different degrees of entrenchment of English within the regional linguistic landscape. At a time when most world Englishes are still maximally represented via one relatively general corpus for feature descriptions rooted in national boundaries, this rich and varied corpus environment enables the empirical depiction of potentially internally regionalised usage patterns for IndE, addressing the following questions: To what extent can we use the term 'Indian English', which suggests a monolithic view (or at least a set of core features) of the variety, and to what extent is the plural 'Indian Englishes' (IndEs) more appropriate? To what extent are differences in linguistic features between regional IndEs categorical and to what extent are they rather quantitative in nature?

This Element is structured as follows. Section 2 establishes the sociolinguistic profiles of regional IndEs. The section begins with an overview of the typological unity and diversity of Indian languages. The general division of Indo-Aryan languages in the North and Dravidian languages in the South is an important consideration when addressing to what extent we can speak of one 'Indian English' as opposed to multiple 'Indian Englishes', since, in addition to other forms of stratification (e.g. between urban and rural), the language contact scenarios and historical entrenchment of English differ substantially at the macro- and micro-levels. In addition, the section highlights language policies of individual states with respect to English on the one hand and local languages on the other. Finally, the section zooms in on the sociolinguistic, typological, and political profiles of regional IndEs as they are represented in the corpora used for the study.

These corpora are the focus of Section 3 on the methodology of our Element. Building on the sociolinguistic profiles introduced in Section 2, this section explains the rationale behind creating the corpora that form the basis of our case studies, namely SAVE2020 and CORINNE. While SAVE2020 samples supra-regional, educated English in numerous South Asian countries, CORINNE specifically seeks to reflect intra-national regional preferences. This means that, by comparing SAVE2020 and CORINNE, statements can be made about features that have become part of a supra-regional IndE as well as features that are (still) restricted to limited regional contexts.

Sections 4 and 5 contain case studies of unity and diversity in IndEs on the linguistic levels of lexis and morphosyntax. Section 4 on lexis highlights spelling variation based on Peters' *Langscape* project (Peters 2000). More specifically, this section of the Element sheds light on intra-IndE spelling preferences with regard to features such as *e*-deletion (e.g. *judgment* vs. *judgement*), the use of Latinate plural suffixes (e.g. *syllabuses* vs. *syllabi*), and *l*-doubling (e.g. *marvelous* vs. *marvellous*). Furthermore, the section investigates degrees of lexical innovation in IndEs. With the lexemes of the *Oxford English Dictionary* (OED) serving as a baseline for what we regard as the common lexical core of world Englishes, we document both previously unrecorded lexemes as well as lexical innovations competing with already existing forms.

Section 5 provides case studies in morphosyntax. In order to address the question of unity and diversity of IndEs, we investigate mass/count nouns (see Sedlatschek 2009: 230), *only/itself* as focus markers (see Lange 2007), as well as verbs + *about*, which contain what would be regarded as redundant prepositions from a prescriptive perspective (e.g. *discuss about*; see Sethi 2011) as representatives of 'typical' supra-regional features of IndE. In addition, we investigate 'intrusive *as*' as a feature that has been noted as being increasingly frequent not only in IndE but also across South Asian Englishes (SAEs) (Koch et al. 2016; Lange 2016).

Section 6 concludes the Element. In this section, we discuss the implications of the lexical and morphosyntactic analyses for the theoretical framing of IndE in the future: while referring to IndE in the singular is understandable from a practical perspective, researchers should be aware of the regional heterogeneity prevalent in India's varieties of English. In addition, we highlight the methodological side of our analysis: combining national and regional newspapers is invaluable for identifying both pan-Indian and regional lexical and morphosyntactic features.

2 Sociolinguistic Profiles of Regional Indian Englishes

English is India's second official language alongside Hindi, the main language of communication between the central government and individual states (Sharma 2022: 89), the official language of six north-eastern states and eight union territories, the language of higher education and the judiciary, as well as the language of instruction in a wide range of fee-paying schools (see Mohanty 2017). Even though successive governments since independence in 1947 have promoted the use of Hindi as an index of national unity, English continues to serve as the national link language, bridging the gap between the northern Hindi-belt states and the southern Dravidian states (see Section 2.1 and Section 2.4 for more details). The story of English in India has been told many times and need not be reiterated here; recent overviews are Mukherjee and Bernaisch (2020) and Lange (2020). Both these accounts frame the history of English in India in the five stages of Schneider's dynamic model of the evolution of PCEs (Schneider 2007). The model proposes a uniform trajectory for PCEs in which stage 4, endonormative stabilisation, marks the emergence of a national variety in its own right. The speech community's self-awareness and linguistic self-confidence have to precede the possible final stage 5, dialect differentiation: without an endonormative standard as the overarching norm, deviation from the standard – that is, variation – cannot be imbued with social meaning. Both of the historical accounts just mentioned describe IndE as moving towards endonormative stabilisation, but not decisively so:

> Although Indian English can thus be viewed as a largely endonormatively stabilized variety in its own right, the present-day situation is also characterized by some remnants of the nativization phase. For example, one can still

find many exponents of what Kachru (2005) has repeatedly labelled *linguistic schizophrenia*, that is, the fact that many competent Indian users of English accept English as an integral part of their linguistic repertoire but at the same time reject the local variant of English at hand once they become aware of the differences between British and Indian English. (Mukherjee and Bernaisch 2020: 170)

Schneider's model focusses on the development of national varieties of English, and so do the ICE corpora, which sample the educated standard(ising) variety of English in the case of second-language (L2) countries. We want to complement this emphasis on the national level with a comparative regional perspective on IndEs, for several reasons. First of all, Kachru's notion of a 'cline of bilingualism' still holds: for large sections of the affluent urban population, English has become an integral part of the multilingual repertoire. On the other hand, English is and remains a foreign language for an even larger part of the poorer and rural population, to be learned from scratch (see also Section 2.1). Social factors such as caste intertwined with class and the urban/rural divide correlate with access to and proficiency in English across India, but with pronounced regional differences. Language and educational policies of individual states also play an important role for English, as spelt out in Sections 2.2 to 2.6. Secondly, English participates in different contact scenarios across multilingual India; a short sketch of the Indian communicative space follows in Section 2.1, while the subsequent sections include more information about the dominant regional languages. Thus, regional variation across IndEs is only to be expected, even though factors such as language contact are notoriously difficult to pin down as the underlying motivation for a specific innovative IndE feature.

We believe that highlighting the regional diversity of IndE is a valuable addition to current research on IndE as a variety in its own right, but we would also like to use our analysis to return to the question of IndE's position in Schneider's model: how unified, how diverse is IndE? To put it differently, to what extent are the differences between the national and the regional newspaper data qualitative or rather quantitative? Are there specific features that are shared across all data sets, therefore pan-regional and thus tacitly part of an emerging standard? Section 2.9 returns to these questions – which are mainly of concern to the international world Englishes community rather than the IndE speech community. Section 2.1 includes two diverging Indian perspectives on the role of English in India.

2.1 Unity in Diversity: The Indian Communicative Space

'The single most important factor that explains the nature of Indian English is that it functions in the complex multilingual ecology of India' (Sridhar 2020: 245). Part of this complexity arises from the sheer number of languages present:

Table 1 The main language families in India and the number of their speakers according to the latest published census data from 2011.

Statement – 9

Family-wise grouping of the 121 scheduled and non-scheduled languages – 2011

Language families	Number of languages	Persons who returned the languages as their mother tongue	Percentage to total population
1	2	3	4
1. Indo-European			
(a) Indo-Aryan	21	94,50,52,555	78.05
(b) Iranian	1	21,677	0.00
(c) Germanic	1	2,59,678	0.02
2. Dravidian	17	23,78,40,116	19.64
3. Austro-Asiatic	14	1,34,93,080	1.11
4. Tibeto-Burmese	66	1,22,57,382	1.01
5. Semito-Hamitic	1	54,947	0.00
Total	121	1,20,89,79,435	99.85

'Linguistically India is among the most diverse countries in the world' (Mohanty 2019: 329), inheriting and continuing the area's multilingual tradition and ethos:

> Traditional South Asia is characterized by a high degree of long-standing, non-replacive bilingualism, which fosters a high degree of convergence, whether at the local, the regional, or the 'global' South Asian level. What is noteworthy is that convergence appears to be generally bidirectional, and that the number or relative social status of the speakers involved does not seem to play a decisive role. (Hock 2022: 315)

Table 1 captures the current distribution of languages and their speakers across India.[1] Article 343 of the Indian Constitution has assigned Hindi the status of official and English the status of second or associate official language; a further twenty-two languages are listed in the Eighth Schedule. These are mostly official state languages, but also include Sanskrit, the classical language of India.[2] The language section of the latest Indian Census from 2011 only provides data for languages with more than 10,000 speakers and recognises the scheduled as well as ninety-nine non-scheduled languages. However, these

---

[1] 'Germanic' (listed as 1c) refers to English. The fifth group, Semito-Hamitic, represents Arabic.
[2] See https://legislative.gov.in/constitution-of-india.

figures represent a considerable degree of abstraction: a 'language' such as Hindi may subsume more than fifty individual 'mother tongues'.

The Indo-Aryan (IA) language family comprises languages such as Hindi with a share of 46.36 per cent across India according to the 2011 census, Urdu (4.19 per cent), Bengali (8.03 per cent), or Marathi (6.86 per cent), and covers the large majority of speakers, mainly in the North of India. Dravidian (DR) languages are dominant in the South of India, with languages such as Telugu (6.7 per cent), Tamil (5.7 per cent), Kannada (3.61 per cent), or Malayalam (2.88 per cent). Language contact between IA and DR over millennia has given rise to a range of convergence features, for example 'a dental-retroflex contrast, Subject Object Verb (SOV) order, and the use of converbs and quotatives' (Hock 2022: 299). The two remaining language families, Austro-Asiatic (AA) and Tibeto-Burmese (TB), together account for only around 2.5 million speakers but for two-thirds of the languages recognised by the census.

The AA language family extends across South and South-East Asia. 'Indeed, more languages of the family are spoken outside the region than within it' (Asher 2008: 41). Khasi with around 1.4 million speakers is mostly spoken in Meghalaya. The speakers of Santali, the only scheduled language in the family, with a share of 0.61 per cent, are mainly located in East India, and another member of this language family is Nicobarese, with around 29,000 speakers on the Nicobar Islands.

The TB language family displays the most striking inverse relationship between the number of languages and their speakers: around 1 per cent of the Indian population speak sixty-six different languages. The TB languages have their origin in the North and North-East of India (see Section 2.3). Lushai/Mizo is the official language of Mizoram; the only scheduled TB languages are Bodo and Manipuri.

This multilingual communicative space has been influenced by 'three major linguistic impacts, those of Sanskritization, Persianization, and Englishization' (Kachru 2008: 2) consecutively. The societal and political responses to these influences have resulted in a range of language policies that came into effect after independence. We shall briefly sketch the most relevant and prominent of these in turn, with a focus on the role of English.

First, the linguistic reorganisation of states following independence answered to a demand that had been raised by the Indian National Congress since 1920 (Schwartzberg 2009: 139). Upon independence, India consisted of a patchwork of colonial administrative regions which were formerly under direct British rule, such as the presidencies of Bengal, Madras, and Bombay. There were further a host of so-called princely states, such as Hyderabad, with less direct interference. These arbitrary administrative divisions, a legacy of colonial power over centuries, were to be redrawn to create federal states which united speech communities with a common language. By and large, the process has been successful (see Schwartzberg 2009 for details). However, it is important to point out that there is no single Indian state which is monolingual with respect to the regional language. In states such as West Bengal or Tamil Nadu, the state's official language may be the mother tongue of the large majority of the population, but linguistic minorities and internal migration will always foster multilingualism of the kind depicted in Fig. 2. The mirror image are the north-eastern states, which are so linguistically diverse that most opted for English as the official state language. Recent processes of state formation (e.g. the secession of Telangana from Andhra Pradesh in the South) were not language-based, but driven by conflicts over unequal access to resources.

Second, the question of a national/official language for independent India was hotly debated in the Indian Constituent Assembly (see Austin 2009). The original article 343 of the Indian constitution made Hindi the official language of the Union and stipulated that the use of English was to be discontinued after fifteen years. However, the unease of the non-Hindi-speaking South erupted into unrest and massive riots over months before 1965, the due date for the abolition of English. As a result, the clause requiring the removal of English as the second official language was dropped (see Lange 2010).

Third, the three-language formula (TLF) concerning language teaching in schools was originally developed in 1957 as 'a set of unifying principles in school education' (Mohanty 2019: 332). The formula, revised in 1961, made the following recommendations for the teaching of languages across India:

1. The regional language or the MT [mother tongue] when the latter is different from the regional language;
2. Hindi or any other Indian language in the Hindi speaking areas; and
3. English or any other modern European language. (Mohanty 2019: 332)

However, the visionary aspect of the TLF never got off the ground: the original idea was to bridge the gap between northern and southern states by teaching a (preferably southern) state language as the second language in the Hindi-speaking areas. In practice, many northern states teach Sanskrit rather than a Dravidian language as the second language (Mohanty 2019: 333), and by way of retaliation some southern states do not include Hindi in their school curricula. Moreover, the TLF only applies to government schools; private schools are free with regard to their choice of languages (Mohanty 2019: 333).

Finally, one important factor that is continually contested and negotiated in Indian society has to be mentioned, namely caste. Even though caste has officially been abolished by the Indian constitution, caste and politics related to caste have an enormous impact on society as a whole, and specifically on the education system and thus access to English. Members of the scheduled castes (SC) and scheduled tribes (ST) as well as OBCs (other backward castes) can claim 'protective discrimination otherwise known as reservations' (Deshpande 2018: 228). Such reservations, elaborate quota systems that are a constant matter of public debate and political negotiations, apply to access to higher education and job opportunities in the public sector. For example, if a university has eight PhD positions to fill, then two each will be reserved for SC/ST applicants, while the remaining four are open for all. This extensive programme of affirmative action has improved the lives of millions of people and even created a so-called creamy layer, that is, persons who have benefitted from reservations and are no longer economically 'backward', so that they cannot claim further benefits based on their caste status. Still, caste-based inequality will remain a challenge for Indian society; after all, 'reservations, especially in higher education, can only provide protected entry or formal inclusion – they cannot deliver social justice' (Deshpande 2018: 229). To make an already complex picture even more complex, religion in general is also correlated with literacy and educational success. Literacy among minority religious groups such as Jains and Christians is far higher than the national average but much lower for Muslims.[3]

The integration of English into the Indian communicative space as such is no longer a contested issue – in the twenty-first century, hardly anybody would subscribe to Gandhi's policy of getting rid of English altogether in favour of Hindustani (colloquial Hindi/Urdu) as the sole national language. Rather, comments such as 'We are glad that the British are gone, but it is good that they left us their language' can be heard, confirming that English has indeed become an 'Asian language', 'a liberated English which contains vitality, innovation, linguistic mix, and cultural identity' (Kachru 1998: 106). However, the extent of the restructuring of the communicative space affected by the presence of English can be conceptualised differently. The prominent researcher and campaigner for linguistic minorities A. K. Mohanty has coined the notion of the 'double divide' in Indian multilingualism (e.g. Mohanty 2017). His focus is on the Indian education system and specifically on the needs of children from tribal and/or minority language backgrounds. He sees a double divide within a hierarchically structured communicative space with English and quality English-medium education at the top, followed by the major state languages which are the languages of instruction in vernacular-medium schools. The indigenous tribal/ minority languages and their speakers find themselves at the bottom of the

---

[3] See https://censusindia.gov.in/nada/index.php/catalog/40443.

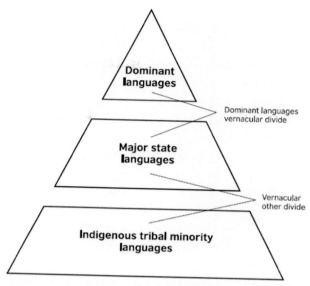

Figure 1 The double divide in multilingual societies.
Figure taken from Mohanty (2017: 269; www.teachingenglish.org.uk/article/multilingu-
alisms-and-development) and reprinted by permission from the British Council.

hierarchy, thus twice removed from English (see Fig. 1). According to Mohanty,
this hierarchy with English as the apex marginalises and alienates pupils from
linguistic minorities as well as those from poorer backgrounds generally.
Mohanty (2017: 269) is very critical of 'the new caste system' which emerges
from the stratified school system, with expensive private high-quality English-
medium (EM) schools at the top, cheaper low-quality EM schools in the middle,
and free vernacular-medium (VM) schools at the bottom:

> With the growing demand among the aspirational lower class parents for EM
> schools, there is now a large number of low cost and low quality EM schools
> in semi-urban, urban slum and rural areas. The quality of teaching-learning
> practices in these schools is extremely poor; teachers are low-paid, lack
> required qualifications and teaching competence and have very low profi-
> ciency in English. . . . generally, in the low cost EM schools children neither
> learn English nor the subject matters and are doomed to failure. (Mohanty
> 2017: 269–70)

It may no longer be accurate to state that the 'majority of realities and lives of
people on the subcontinent are untouched by the presence of English'
(Schneider 2007: 161), since 'between seven and nine years of age, most
children in India show an understanding that English is more prestigious than

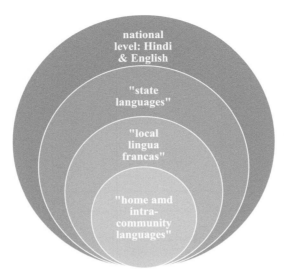

Figure 2 A non-hierarchical model of the Indian communicative space (based on Satyanath 2015: 108).

other languages' (Mohanty 2017: 267). The challenge to foster a more inclusive education system remains, but there are also other points of view in the 'instrumentality vs. identity debate' (Sharma 2022: 88), stressing the liberating potential of English for social mobility.

Shobha Satyanath's conceptualisation of the Indian communicative space is based on her and her associates' research into contemporary multilingual practices in a range of speech communities. She proposes a concentric model (Fig. 2) with up to four levels (Satyanath 2015: 108): the inner circle comprises 'home and intra-community languages'; the second circle with the 'local lingua francas' may be separate from the next level of the 'state languages' but can also be coextensive with it. The outermost national layer comprises Hindi and English. Adding a differentiation between spoken and written language practices, Satyanath concludes:

> Though English has not replaced the local languages, it has replaced literacy in regional languages in major urban areas to a considerable extent due to rising English education ... So, the overall model that India presents is pluralistic, where multiple linguistic and cultural practices coexist without necessarily competing. (2015: 108)

However, there is evidence that the 'traditional pattern of non-replacive bilingualism is now in danger of becoming replaced by a fairly rapid shift to the State Languages in the context of the Linguistic States' (Hock 2022: 315). That is, even if the claim of English as a 'killer language' in the Indian context appears wildly exaggerated, local minority languages are indeed under threat, but by the official state languages.

Table A1 in the Appendix brings together several demographic indicators which play a role for the 'range in terms of functional allocation, and [the] depth in terms of societal penetration' (Kachru 1994: 512–13) of English within each individual state's communicative space, to be included in a more detailed discussion of regional profiles in the following sections.[4] Column 3 lists the overall population of each state together with the percentage of people living in rural versus urban settings. This figure is relevant in our context as urban areas potentially allow for better access to educational facilities and also typically foster the use of English as an intra-national link language. Column 4 depicts the literacy rate per state in the respective mother tongue, differentiated between men's and women's literacy. Illiteracy obviously presents a major obstacle for schooling to begin with, turning the acquisition of English in school into an even more remote option. Moreover, gender disparities in literacy rates highlight larger gender-based inequalities in the respective state. Column 5 presents the percentage of graduates of each state's population, that is, the number of people who have successfully completed higher education, which is always English-medium. The final column includes data from ASER (*Annual State of Education Report*), a survey that has been carried out since 2005 for and as part of Pratham, an Indian NGO devoted to education (Graddol 2010: 80, www.pratham.org/about/). Researchers for the ASER regularly survey the attendance and test the proficiencies of rural school children in several subjects, among them English.

2.2 The North

The North of India is represented in CORINNE by Uttarakhand, a relatively young state carved out of Uttar Pradesh in 2000 following separatist demands. Despite the geographical location close to the Himalayas, the state is often included in the central zone. As Table A1 in the Appendix shows, Uttarakhand is now ahead of Uttar Pradesh in literacy, number of graduates, and rural children's English skills. The area is also famous for engendering and sustaining a highly successful environmentalist agenda: since the 1970s, local villagers led by women protested peacefully against the destruction of forests. The so-called Chipko movement, deriving its name from the Hindi *chipko*, 'to hug, cling to',

---

[4] The main source of information is the 2011 Census of India (available at https://censusindia.gov .in/census.website/data/census-tables).

and thus its non-violent tactics of 'tree-hugging' (www.britannica.com/topic/Chipko-movement), provided inspiration for ecological movements in India and beyond.

2.3 The North-East

The north-eastern states, collectively known as the Seven Sisters (now plus Sikkim as eighth state), share land borders with Chinese-controlled Tibet, Myanmar, Bhutan, and Bangladesh, and are only connected to India via a slim land corridor. Four of the Seven Sisters are represented in CORINNE, namely Arunachal, Meghalaya, Nagaland, and Assam; the former three were originally part of Assam before they were granted more autonomy as independent federal states. As already mentioned, the North-East is India's most diverse linguistic area, mirroring its cultural diversity and also its relative distance from the country's majority Hindu culture. American missionaries were quite successful in spreading Christianity specifically in the mountainous regions, and the tribal culture continues to be an emblem of a local identity. The north-eastern diaspora across India frequently experiences downright racism, and the North-East as a whole has suffered from longstanding armed conflicts between separatist groups and Indian security forces, called 'liberation movements' or 'insurgencies' depending on the respective point of view.

2.4 Central

The large central Hindi belt states are represented in CORINNE by Madhya Pradesh. The state's literacy rate is below the national average, and its results in the ASER survey (see Table A1) are the lowest across all India: only slightly more than a quarter of children in Standard VIII in rural areas can read simple sentences in English. The state hosts some elite universities in its cities, but traditional rural structures in combination with poverty impede access to education for a considerable segment of the population.

2.5 The South

All the Dravidian states are represented in CORINNE, namely Andhra Pradesh, Karnataka, Kerala, Tamil Nadu, and Telangana, which split away from Andhra Pradesh in 2014. The region hosts two of India's major internationally connected commercial hubs, Bengaluru (Bangalore) in Karnataka and Hyderabad in Telangana. Hyderabad is also home to the English and Foreign Languages University (EFL-U, formerly CIEFL), India's foremost institution for research and teacher training concerning English and English language acquisition.

Despite the region's geographical and cultural diversity, one common factor emerges from the shared Dravidian identity: most of the southern states are or have been at some point governed by regional parties in explicit opposition to the national parties. Tamil Nadu, for example, has been ruled since the language riots in the 1960s by one of the parties which includes the label 'Dravidian' in its name. In Kerala, communist parties have continuously shaped the state's political agenda; today, Kerala tops all Indian states on international development indices such as gender equality, high literacy rates, and low infant mortality. English is generally more popular than Hindi as the intra-national link language and receives more support than Hindi in language education in most states.

2.6 The East

According to Schneider's dynamic model, the onset of stage 2, exonormative stabilisation, began with the British gaining control over Bengal and Orissa (now Orya) in the wake of the battle of Plassey in 1757 (Schneider 2007: 163); both states are represented in CORINNE. Bengal with its administrative capital Calcutta (now Kolkata) thus became the 'British bridgehead' (see Marshall 1988) for further territorial expansion. A considerable section of the local elite profited financially from their association with the British; the Bengali civil society actively engaged with the new language of power and the new literary and scholarly perspectives that came with it. A prominent person in this context was Ram Mohan Roy, a public intellectual and leading figure in the so-called Bengal Renaissance (see Kopf 1969). In a sense, then, English became an integral part of the linguistic landscape in Bengal much earlier than in India overall.

2.7 The West

The three states Gujarat, Maharashtra, and Goa represent the West in CORINNE. Portuguese forts and trading posts along the western coast predated the arrival of their English competitors. However, these were subsequently taken over by the British, including the port of Bombay (now Mumbai) in 1665 (Dalrymple 2019: 22–3). Goa remained under Portuguese rule until it was forcefully integrated into independent India in 1961.[5] Today, Goa is known as a popular intra- and international holiday destination, favouring the extended use of English.

Maharashtra is the second-most populous Indian state after Uttar Pradesh (Central). Due to their economic strength, Maharashtra and especially its capital

---

[5] See www.britannica.com/place/Goa/History.

Mumbai are the destination of choice for large-scale internal labour migration. Many local and international companies are represented in the 'golden triangle' Mumbai-Nashik-Pune, taking advantage of the region's modern infrastructure and skilled work force. Greater Mumbai with a population of more than 20 million hosts both the Bollywood film industry and many of its superstars as well as South Asia's largest slum, Dharavi, which gained international prominence with the movie *Slumdog Millionaire* from 2008.[6] There is tentative evidence for a supra-local IndE accent emerging from Mumbai: according to research by Maxwell et al. (2021: 11), '[p]eople from the large urban centre of Mumbai were identified as having a "very neutral" accent: Mumbai being the place where "every-one . . . speaks normal English"'.

Gujarat, Mahatma Gandhi's home state as well as the home state of the current prime minister Narendra Modi, has a lower overall literacy rate than both Goa and Maharashtra, but is catching up in terms of economic development. The coastal city of Surat is known to all scholars of SAEs as the first outpost of the British East India Company on Indian soil, founded in 1612 (Schneider 2007: 162). Today, Surat is better known as the world's leading centre for diamond cutting and polishing.

2.8 Union Territories

The label 'union territory' is basically an administrative designation, indicating that the respective area is under central administration. Two rather diverse union territories are covered by CORINNE: the northern state Jammu and Kashmir bordering on Pakistan and violently contested between the two hostile South Asian neighbours, and the Andaman and Nicobar group of islands off the south-eastern coast of India. Everyday life in Jammu and Kashmir has been severely disrupted by separatist terrorist attacks and Indian military rule for decades, with negative impact on agriculture, trade, and tourism, to name but a few areas. Incidentally, the scheduled language Kashmiri with around 6.7 million speakers in the state is the only IA language which does not have SOV as its basic word order, but rather verb-second as in German (Masica 1993: 335–6).

The Andaman and Nicobar Islands are one of the smallest Indian states in terms of population: fewer than half a million people live on the thirty-eight inhabited islands in the archipelago consisting of 838 islands.[7] One of these, North Sentinel Island, is the home of a small and secluded Andamanese tribal group, the Sentinelese, and has been declared off-limits to all visitors by the Indian government. The current linguistic diversity on the islands derives from

---

[6] See www.imdb.com/title/tt1010048/.
[7] See www.andaman.gov.in/.

migration; speakers of Bengali, Hindi, and a range of South Indian languages vastly outnumber the speakers of indigenous languages such as Nicobarese (AA). The capital Port Blair is the only major town, providing intra- and international connectivity through its airport.

2.9 Outlook: Towards a Standard Indian English?

While Section 2.1 gave a general overview of the Indian communicative space, the position of English within it, and the parameters of variation in the range and depth of English, Sections 2.2 to 2.8 together with Table A1 in the Appendix could do no more than sketch some of the regional differences that are bound to affect the use of English in the respective states. The degree of entrenchment of English in a specific state may be due to different reasons: English may be more widely used because it is the state language, as in the linguistically highly diverse north-eastern states, or because it is preferred over Hindi as the intranational link language, as in the southern states below the Hindi belt. English may be a foreign rather than a second language for poorer sections of the population who live in rural areas with limited access to well-funded education, or it may be taken for granted by large batches of college students in metropolitan areas. Still, specific regional differences are likely to be reflected in specific regional usages, as Sections 4 and 5 will spell out. However, regional differentiation should not be taken to indicate stage 5 in Schneider's dynamic model, that is, differentiation as the final stage following stage 4 of endonormative stabilisation, which includes standardisation. As mentioned earlier, IndE has not been codified yet, thus lacking one of the crucial indicators of endonormative stabilisation. However, several recent attitude studies hint at a tacit acceptance of some IndE norms even if they clash with British English (BrE), as well as an increasing linguistic self-confidence. A study by Doibale et al. (forthc.) queried respondents about their preference for either a standard BrE expression or an innovative but 'incorrect' IndE alternative. Generally, the influence of prescriptive usage guides adhering to a BrE standard is waning, specifically in the field of lexical choices: IndE forms such as *prepone, matchbox* (rather than *box of matches*), or *to pass out* in the sense of 'to graduate' enjoy overwhelming support. Maxwell et al.'s (2021: 12) attitude study among a group of young urban professionals reveals 'a growing sense of linguistic security' together with a 'growing sense of ownership of the English language in India'. However, there is still the 'pressing need in English-language teaching in India today. . .for a methodologically sound and linguistically sophisticated grammar of educated Indian English that would be considered both authentically

Indian and nationally and internationally intelligible' (Sridhar 2020: 271). One of the aims of this study is to contribute new data to the question of how such a grammar could actually look like.

3 Methodology

Varieties of IndE have been represented in multiple corpora, first in the *Kolhapur Corpus of Indian English* (Shastri et al. 1986) and later in the Indian component of ICE (Greenbaum & Nelson 1996). The *Kolhapur Corpus* is part of the 'Brown family' of corpora and, as such, comprises written language across a range of text types in the categories 'Informative Prose' and 'Imaginative Prose'. In contrast, the IndE component of ICE features both spoken and written language and covers various text types in both modes of communication (see chapter 4 in Lange and Leuckert 2020 for an overview). Both corpora represent important resources in the study of IndE. However, ICE-India in particular has been used extensively in research on grammatical (e.g. Lange 2012; Leuckert 2019; Suárez-Gómez & Seoane 2021) and, more recently, pragmatic (e.g. Degenhardt & Bernaisch 2022; Funke 2022) variation. In addition to containing a sizable portion of spoken language and metadata for most components, a major advantage of ICE is the comparable structure of the sub-corpora: all of them contain approximately one million words and all of them follow the same structure, since all of them are compiled with the overarching goal of comparability in mind. However, the diachronic dimension introduced by the long time frame of the ICE project (Hundt 2015) means that direct comparability may be limited depending on the corpora used. Other aspects to consider are the relatively small size of the individual ICE components and, most importantly for the study at hand, that they do not allow for differentiated analyses of the supra-regional versus regional continuum.

In our investigation of intra-varietal heterogeneity in the lexis and morpho-syntax of IndE, we compare selected lexical and morphosyntactic phenomena in SAVE2020 and CORINNE. The SAVE corpora, namely SAVE2020 and its predecessor SAVE2011 (Bernaisch et al. 2011), and CORINNE differ from ICE in significant ways. They only contain written language and have a much bigger word count but, most importantly, they were created with other goals in mind: the SAVE corpora contain acrolectal newspaper language from six SAEs, allowing for in-depth comparisons specifically of these varieties. CORINNE, in turn, contains regional newspapers to make comparisons of mesolectal language from different parts of India possible, thus providing access to potential regional variation.

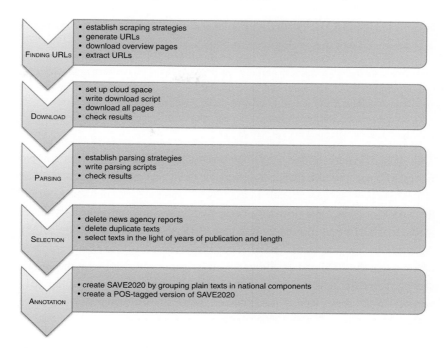

FINDING URLs
- establish scraping strategies
- generate URLs
- download overview pages
- extract URLs

DOWNLOAD
- set up cloud space
- write download script
- download all pages
- check results

PARSING
- establish parsing strategies
- write parsing scripts
- check results

SELECTION
- delete news agency reports
- delete duplicate texts
- select texts in the light of years of publication and length

ANNOTATION
- create SAVE2020 by grouping plain texts in national components
- create a POS-tagged version of SAVE2020

Figure 3 Corpus compilation, processing, and annotation of SAVE2020 (from Bernaisch et al. 2021: 4).

In the following sections, we introduce SAVE2020 and CORINNE with regard to the background of their compilation, their word counts, and the newspapers featured in them. In addition, we comment on our approach to getting at the unity and diversity of IndEs.

3.1 SAVE2020

The SAEs covered by SAVE2020 are Bangladeshi, Indian, Maldivian, Nepali, Pakistani, and Sri Lankan English, with about three million words per variety. For each variety, contributions to two newspapers amounting to about 1.5 million words per newspaper were sampled. The Indian SAVE component contains texts from *The Statesman* and *The Times of India* published between 2019 and 2020.[8] The procedure of building the SAVE corpora is visualised in Fig. 3.

SAVE2020 has been tagged using *TagAnt* (Anthony 2015) and the corpus is available in plain text or POS-tagged (Bernaisch et al. 2021: 4). Considering the

---

[8] In corpus examples, we use the abbreviations 'TS' for *The Statesman* and 'ToI' for *The Times of India*.

objectives behind SAVE, both SAVE2020 and its predecessor from 2011 represent acrolectal newspaper Englishes in South Asia:

> The texts included in the 18-million-word SAVE Corpus have been produced by highly proficient users and have undergone several rounds of editing so that deviances from native Englishes in the Kachruvian Inner Circle cannot be viewed as learner mistakes, but as results of a process of structural nativisation. (Bernaisch et al. 2014: 11)

This design feature of the SAVE corpora is particularly important for our Element, since the newspaper language in them represents a supra-regional standard and hence corresponds to the 'unity' component of our study. So far, the SAVE corpora have primarily been used in research on morphosyntactic features of SAEs (e.g. Bernaisch & Lange 2012; Koch et al. 2016; Götz 2022). An important innovation of the SAVE corpora in comparison to other corpora of SAEs is that the 2020 update allows for investigations of short-term diachronic change, since the new version is based on the same newspapers as the 2011 version. In the remainder of the Element, SAVE2020 is meant to refer to the Indian sub-corpus of SAVE2020 unless specified otherwise.

3.2 CORINNE

The SAVE corpora have opened the door to meaningful analyses and comparisons of acrolectal, supra-regional SAEs. In contrast to the objectives behind the creation of SAVE, CORINNE's main goal is to 'represent an additional level of language between the local spoken language and the national printed language' (Yurchenko et al. 2021a: 182), which is why the corpus features exclusively regional newspapers. CORINNE is mainly composed of news reports and articles but also features editorials, op-eds, and letters to the editor. The criteria for a newspaper to be included in CORINNE are that

1. It must be based and mainly circulated in the state it is said to represent;
2. It must have a category reporting on local (state/city) news;
3. It must have a print version; however, exceptions can be made if only online newspapers for the state are available;
4. It must be 'scrapable' using our web crawling script . . .;
5. Ideally, it should also contain a non-news articles category, such as editorials, op-eds, letters to the editor, etc. (Yurchenko et al. 2021a: 184)

The included newspapers, their regions and states of dissemination, as well as the categories and total word counts for CORINNE are listed in Table 2. The table also shows the region abbreviations that we use in the following sections.

Table 2 Structure and components of CORINNE (Yurchenko et al. 2021b).

Region	State	Newspaper	Time span	Categories	Total words
Centre (C)	Madhya Pradesh	*Central Chronicle*	2018–2020	News (730,539)	730,539
East (E)	Odisha	*Orissa POST*	2015–2020	News (1,596,042)	1,596,042
	West Bengal	*Kolkata 24x7*	2015–2019	News (1,520,994)	1,520,994
North (N)	Uttarakhand	*Garhwal Post*	2018–2020	News (1,064,913) Editorials + Features (442,284)	1,507,197
North-East (NE)	Arunachal	*The Arunachal Times*	2017–2020	News (1,033,899) Editorials (555,927)	1,589,826
	Assam	*The Assam Tribune*	2014–2019	News (1,514,147)	1,514,147
	Meghalaya	*The Shillong Times*	2016–2020	News (1,175,744) Editorial (475,281)	1,651,025
	Nagaland	*The Morung Express* *Nagaland Post*	2014; 2019 (ME) 2019–2020 (NP)	News (953,545) Editorial + Public Space (590,857)	1,544,402
South (S)	Andhra Pradesh	*The Hans India*	2015–2020	News (1,508,659)	1,508,659
	Karnataka	*Star of Mysore*	2017–2020	News (1,145,767) Editorial (425,173)	1,570,849
	Kerala	*Madhyamam*	2019–2021	News (774,471) Opinion (438,861)	1,213,332
	Tamil Nadu	*News Today*	2018–2020	News (1,560,311)	1,560,311

Table 2 (cont.)

Region	State	Newspaper	Time span	Categories	Total words
	Telangana	*Telangana Today*	2017–2020	News (1,072,726) Editorial + Opinion (448,854)	1,521,580
West (W)	Goa	*The Navhind Times*	2020	News (1,192,077) Opinion (336,528)	1,528,605
	Gujarat	*Ahmedabad Mirror*	2015–2020	News (1,585,969)	1,585,969
	Maharashtra	*Lokmat*	2020–2021 (L)	News (1,107,128)	1,516,085
		The Bridge Chronicle	2017–2020 (BC)	Opinion (408,957)	
Union Territories (UT)[9]	Andaman & Nicobar	*Andaman Sheekha*	2015–2020	News (1,599,277)	1,599,277
	Jammu & Kashmir	*Kashmir Observer*	2015–2020	News (1,074,181) In Depth (558,988)	1,633,169
	NCT Delhi	*New Delhi Times*	2015–2020	News (688,640)	688,640
				Total	27,580,648

[9] For some analyses, we specify the region in the abbreviation (UT-AN for Andaman and Nicobar and UT-JK for Jammu and Kashmir).

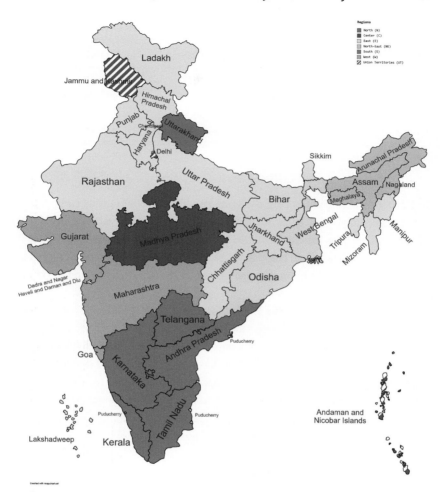

Figure 4 Colour-coded regional map of India showing the states and Union Territories featured in CORINNE.[10]

Fig. 4 shows a colour-coded map of India, with the regions encompassing the states and Union Territories that are part of CORINNE highlighted in different colours.

The first case study based on CORINNE is introduced in Yurchenko et al. (2021a) and compares the 'intrusive *as*'-construction in the sub-corpora for Tamil Nadu and Uttarakhand. We discuss this construction in more detail in a follow-up study later in this Element.

---

[10] This map was created with mapchart.net and is used under a CC-BY-SA 4.0 license.

Table 3 Comparison of SAVE2020 and CORINNE.

	SAVE2020	**CORINNE**
Word Count	3,000,005	27,580,648
Time Frame	2019–2020	2015–2020[11]
Type of Language	acrolectal	mesolectal
Range and Coverage	supra-regional	regional

3.3 Summary and Comparison of CORINNE and SAVE2020

Both corpora were created with the same key principles of corpus compilation in mind and important steps were taken specifically to weed out irrelevant information, such as articles provided by news agencies and doublets. Table 3 summarises our dataset and compares SAVE2020 and CORINNE with regard to word count, covered time frame, type of language, and the range and coverage of the newspapers.

It is important to note that the labels 'acrolectal' and 'mesolectal' in the table are generalisations, since the individual newspapers may differ from each other in particular as far as the degree of copy-editing, revision, and other factors are concerned. Moreover, while CORINNE has a larger total word count than the Indian components of the SAVE corpora, the individual sub-sections of CORINNE are smaller with about 1.5 million words per state. Overall, we believe that the two corpora represent an ideal basis for a comparison of supra-regional and regional IndE newspaper language.

3.4 Feature Selection and Analysis

A key challenge in identifying differences between supra-regionally nativised or nativising features on the one hand and emerging regional features or idiosyncratic usages on the other hand lies in the fact that our knowledge of IndE and other varieties is deeply informed by 'what we know'. Certain features, no matter the linguistic level, are considered typical of the variety and, thus, tend to also be addressed in new publications on IndE. This 'feature-list approach' (Sedlatschek 2009: chapter 2) is, of course, not inherently wrong, and what is done and how it is done should mainly be decided based on the research goals of a given project. However, such an approach limits the scope and may therefore lead to a myopic perspective that disregards emerging phenomena. We address this issue by combining a corpus-based with a corpus-driven approach (Tognini-Bonelli 2001): in addition to updating our

---

[11] For selected newspapers, the time frame was expanded in order to reach the word count.

knowledge of features that are well-known parts of IndE lexis and morpho-syntax, we also consider new forms and features that we identified during data exploration. In this Element, we opted for a complementation of lexical and lexicogrammatical objects of investigation. Word and spelling choices – particularly when it comes to innovative vocabulary items – as presented in Sections 4.1 to 4.3 may be expected to attract more linguistic attention and might thus more strongly provide transparent insights into what speakers regard as locally acceptable standards in comparison to lexicogrammatical routines. At the same time, these probably less conscious lexicogrammatical routines have been profiled as salient in the evolutionary localisation of postcolonial Englishes (Schneider 2007), which is why we studied a selection of features particularly relevant to the Indian context in Sections 5.1 to 5.4.

For the lexical and morphosyntactic case studies, we conducted analyses of selected features mainly using *AntConc* (Anthony 2022) and *R* (R Core Team 2022). More details on the employed methods are provided as part of the individual case studies.

4 Lexis

This section studies the lexis of contemporary IndEs from various angles. In Section 4.1, spelling preferences are observed across a number of orthographic alternants; in Section 4.2, the lexical choices by IndE speakers are functionally modelled and compared as evident from insights derived from multidimensional analyses suggested by Biber (1988), and, in Section 4.3, so far unrecorded lexical innovations in IndEs are documented and described – particularly regarding their semantics and distribution across the individual IndEs covered.

4.1 Spelling in IndEs

Rooted in the existence of 'divergent areas of editorial style for British and American writers and publishers' (Peters 2001: 9), spelling preferences of speakers across all three Kachruvian Circles were – among other structural features – surveyed in 1998/1999 in the framework of *Langscape*, a project jointly coordinated by Cambridge University Press, *English Today*, and Pam Peters to provide an empirical basis for the then forthcoming *Cambridge Guide to English Usage* (Peters 2004). More specifically, the lexical analyses of *Langscape* (see Peters 2000: 37) established groups for orthographic alternants and a selection of alternants that could be studied meaningfully with corpus-linguistic methods and be used to understand spelling preferences in present-day IndEs: (a) the addition/ omission of letters such as *a* (e.g. *aesthetic* vs. *esthetic*), *e* (*ageing* vs. *aging*), and *o* (*homoeopathy* vs. *homeopathy*); (b) the doubling of the consonant *l* (e.g. *labeled* vs. *labelled*); (c) the usage of Latinate as opposed to English morphs (e.g. *fungi* vs. *funguses*); (d) the usage of punctuation after abbreviated forms (e.g. *etc* vs. *etc.*).[12] Said spelling differences offer various strands of interpretation. The addition versus the omission of the letters *a*, *e*, and *o* as well as the doubling of the consonant *l* may be indicative of tendencies towards more complex, and possibly convoluted or even archaic spelling styles as opposed to simpler, more accessible ones. The choice between Latinate plural suffixes and non-Latinate ones may represent writers' inclinations to employ conservative in contrast to innovative spelling and a small group of variants also represents the American English (AmE) versus BrE divide.

After a list of relevant items had been culled from Peters (2000, 2001), concordances with the respective spelling variants were drawn from the regional components of CORINNE and SAVE2020. Subsequently, irrelevant hits (e.g. *reveled* – alternating with *revelled* – not used as a word form of REVEL, but a misspelt word form of REVEAL or *through* – alternating with *thru* – as a misspelling of *though*) were discarded. Table 4 provides a summary of the different groups of orthographic alternants, the number of pairs of orthographic alternants – for example *millenniums* versus *millennia* for Latinate versus English morphs – per group and the total number of corpus examples retained for each orthographic alternation.

Subsequently, the absolute frequencies of occurrence for each pair of orthographic alternants (e.g. JUDGMENT vs. JUDGEMENT for the group of addition/ omission of *e*) were used to devise pairwise relative frequencies for each corpus component investigated.[13] With the intention of visualising central spelling trends across the corpus components as in Fig. 5 for the absence/presence of *a*, the means of relative frequencies have been calculated as follows. In the case of the addition/omission of *a*, twelve pairs of orthographic alternants (e.g. *archaeology* vs. *archeology* or *mediaeval* vs. *medieval*) have been examined and their absolute and relative frequencies documented. To derive overall spelling trends for the individual corpus components across the individual orthographic alternations listed in Table 4, the mean relative frequencies of both alternants – for example

---

[12] For a full list of spelling features examined in the *Langscape* project, please refer to Peters (2000, 2001). For the hierarchical cluster analyses and the resulting dendrogram in Fig. 11, a miscellaneous category of other orthographically variable forms was also included, but it is not discussed separately since it – unlike the other groups discussed here – amalgamates different spelling contrasts (e.g. *colour* vs. *color*, but also *through* vs. *thru*).

[13] For instance, in COR-UT forms of JUDGMENT occurred with an absolute frequency of 156 and forms of JUDGEMENT 51 times. Consequently, JUDGMENT (75.36%) is the dominant spelling variant compared to JUDGEMENT (24.64%) in COR-UT.

Table 4 Orthographic alternations and absolute number of corpus examples.

Orthographic alternation	Number of pairs of orthographic alternations studied	Absolute number of corpus examples retained for analysis
Addition/omission of *a*	12	712
Addition/omission of *e*	40	2,156
Addition/omission of *o*	5	433
Doubling of *l*	14	545
Latinate vs. English morphs	5	108
Addition/omission of punctuation	26	53,773

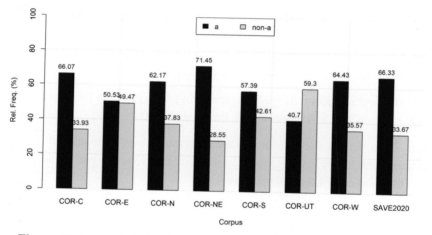

Figure 5 Means of relative frequencies of spelling variants with added or omitted *a*.

the mean relative frequency of added *a* versus the mean relative frequency of omitted *a* – were calculated per corpus component.[14] The respective means for the absence or presence of *a* in the single corpus components are shown in Fig. 5.

---

[14] In this calculation, each pair of orthographic alternants – in case one of their forms is attested at least once in the corpus data – has an equally large impact on the mean relative frequency in the sense that the respective relative frequencies per pair of orthographic alternants are added up and then divided by the number of pairs of orthographic alternants. This was necessary because there was the tendency of some pairs of orthographic alternants to dominate certain orthographic alternations. Consider, for instance, the orthographic alternation addition/omission of

The distribution of forms with or without *a* across the individual corpus components is statistically highly significant ($\chi^2 = 23.238$, df = 7, $p < 0.01$, Cramer's $V = 0.181$).[15] Still, seven out of eight corpus components are similar in that spelling variants featuring *a* on average outnumber forms without *a*, which is generally in line with the preference by mainly Inner Circle speakers of English (56% with *a* vs. 44% without *a*) reported in Peters (2001). In the IndE data, this tendency of adding rather than omitting *a* appears most pronounced in COR-NE (71.45% with *a* vs. 28.55% without *a*), SAVE2020 (66.33% with *a* vs. 33.67% without *a*), and COR-C (66.07% with *a* vs. 33.93% without *a*), while COR-E (50.53% with *a* vs. 49.47% without *a*) shows only a comparatively minute preference for forms with as opposed to without *a*. COR-UT (40.7% with *a* vs. 59.3% without *a*) is the only component that stands in categorical opposition to the others in that alternants without *a* are preferred. As regards the individual pairs of orthographic alternants, the corpus components uniformly feature more instances of *aesthetic* as in (1) compared to their *a*-less forms, but *medieval* as in (2) is dominant in each corpus component studied – more specifically, *mediaeval* is only attested once in COR-NE (see example (3)) in the entire corpus environment.

(1) Presence of huge, magnificent trees itself gives simple pleasure in our minds and aesthetic feeling. <COR-NE-Assam_City_2016–11.txt>

(2) The land's kings of the medieval times may have rested in the pages of history, . . . <COR-S-Karnataka_SM_Editorial_02.txt>

(3) . . . the Sultans, the Badshahs or the European powers, who entered the Brahmaputra Valley in the mediaeval period, were lured to this part of the globe <COR-NE-Assam_City_2018–04.txt>

Statistically significant differences across the corpus components can also be attested with regard to the occurrence or absence of *e* in the orthographic alternants ($\chi^2 = 95.908$, df = 7, $p < 0.001$, Cramer's $V = 0.211$). Fig. 6 displays

---

punctuation: Out of its total of 53,773 examples, 34,888 examples, that is, roughly two out of three, were examples of *Dr* versus *Dr.* and *Prof* versus *Prof.* In case one would have allowed this quantitative dominance of *Dr* versus *Dr.* and *Prof* versus *Prof* to be accounted for in the mean relative frequencies, they would not have produced a balanced picture across all of the pairs of orthographic alternants studied, but rather only a depiction of trends of the dominant *Dr* versus *Dr.* and *Prof* versus *Prof.*

[15] In case its assumptions with regard to absolute and expected frequencies of occurrence are met, Pearson's (1900) chi-square test is employed for monofactorial statistical testing and the chi-square value, degrees of freedom, the significance level, and Cramer's *V* ranging from 0 to 1 as a measure of effect size not biased by sample size are reported. When chi-square assumptions are not met, Fisher's (1922) exact test is used instead. Both tests cannot capture the multifactorial nature of linguistic choices (see Gries 2018), but can serve as first indications whether noteworthy differences between the individual IndEs may exist in the absence of research that has profiled other factors as indispensable in spelling choices.

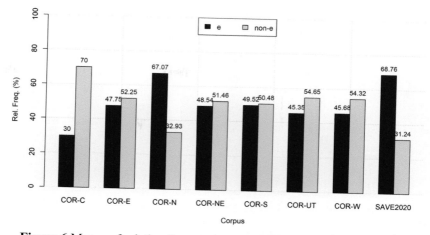

Figure 6 Means of relative frequencies of spelling variants with added or omitted *e*.

that, with the exception of COR-N (67.07% with *e* vs. 32.93% without *e*) and SAVE2020 (68.76% with *e* vs. 31.24% without *e*), which show a marked preference for alternants featuring *e*, forms without *e* tend to be slightly preferred in the remaining corpus components, while *e*-less forms dominate most notably in COR-C (30% with *e* vs. 70% without *e*). By means of comparison, writers largely from the Inner Circle (Peters 2001) rather opt for adding *e* than leaving it out (64% with *e* vs. 36% without *e*). Still, it is not surprising that spelling preferences regarding individual items by default vary across the IndE corpus components, but spelling choices conform in a shared tendency towards forms with *e* for *eyeing* as in (4) or *e*-less variants for *usable* as in (5).

(4) Then we cruised back on the old Rajpur Road, which was mostly downhill, with me <u>eyeing</u> all the lovely houses enroute <COR-N-Uttarakhand_Feature_02 .txt>

(5) The team also recovered huge amounts of spices which were not in <u>usable</u> condition as per the expiry dates mentioned in the packets. <COR-NE-Assam_City_2019–05.txt>

The absence or presence of *o* in the spelling alternants examined as in Fig. 7 profiles two groups of corpus components – differences across corpus components are statistically significant ($\chi^2 = 22.957$, df = 7, $p < 0.01$, Cramer's $V = 0.23$). Forms featuring *o* represent default choices in COR-NE (81.32% with *o* vs. 18.68% without *o*), COR-S (56.5% with *o* vs. 43.5% without *o*), COR-UT (51.13% with *o* vs. 48.87% without *o*), and COR-W (64.13% with *o* vs. 35.87%

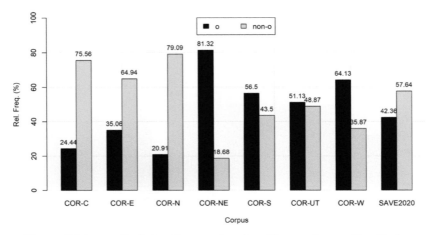

Figure 7 Means of relative frequencies of spelling variants with added or omitted *o*.

without *o*), which is in line with mainly Inner Circle speaker preferences (61% with *o* vs. 39% without *o*; Peters 2001). Still, in COR-C (24.44% with *o* vs. 75.56% without *o*), COR-E (35.06% with *o* vs. 64.94% without *o*), COR-N (20.91% with *o* vs. 79.09% without *o*), and SAVE2020 (42.36% with *o* vs. 57.64% without *o*), *o*-less forms prevail notably, representing an overall lower degree of spelling uniformity in IndEs with this set of orthographic alternants. With a view to the individual lexical items studied, there are no examples where spelling preferences are stable across corpus components – the *o*-featuring variant *diarrhoea* as in (6) is more frequent than its *o*-less counterpart in each corpus part to the exception of COR-UT and SAVE2020, where both forms occur equally frequently. Similarly, most corpus parts conform in that the *o*-less variant *homeopathy* as in (7) is the default choice, but *homoeopathy* is the more frequent variant in COR-NE and COR-UT.

(6) ... more than 80 devotees, who had consumed Tomato Bath, took ill, complaining of vomiting and <u>diarrhoea</u> and a burning sensation in eyes and stomach [...] <COR-S-Karnataka_SM_News_03.txt>

(7) Allied courses like dental surgery, physiotherapy, ayurveda and <u>homeopathy</u> have significantly higher number of girls. <COR-W-Gujarat_News_Coverstory_02. txt>

As a means of interim summary regarding the absence or presence of *a*, *e*, and *o*, heterogeneity characterises spelling choices with the individual IndEs. This heterogeneity can be observed from various angles: (a) with a view to the individual spelling features studied so far in isolation, the preferences for absence/presence of *a*, *e*, or *o* did not hold uniformly across all corpus components studied (although *e* and particularly *a* absence/presence appeared more consistent across IndEs than *o* absence/presence); (b) with a view to individual corpus parts, *a*, *e*, and *o* orthographic variants were systematically variable in the sense that consistent patterns of absence or presence of the letters studied could not be observed for any corpus part studied, for example while COR-C prefers the presence *a*, spelling variants with *e* or *o* are dispreferred; and (c) each of the distributions of *a*, *e*, and *o* spelling variants triggers statistically significant differences across the corpus parts studied.

In case the realisation of the letters concerned is considered indicative of a more complex or convoluted style, then this characterisation would only relatively generally hold for the addition/omission of *a* in IndE, although it is to be noted that this preference for *a*-realisation is shared with Inner Circle writers of English. While native writers of English also tend towards the inclusion of *e* in contexts where it is optional, most IndE corpus components at hand do not follow this trend. Also, in terms of the realisation of *o* the data do not warrant profiling IndE writers' spelling styles as more complex or convoluted than that of Inner Circle writers of English. Given that Peters (2001) summarises that Inner Circle members more often than not realise *a*, *e*, and *o*, the present-day spelling routines within IndE actually appear less complex or convoluted than those of the Inner Circle, although the region-specific variation of IndE with regard to said spelling features as well as the temporal distance of Peters' (2001) study must not be disregarded.

In terms of the doubling of the letter *l* (Fig. 8), the heterogeneity across IndEs is also evident from varying categorical preferences across corpus components, which yield statistically significant differences ($\chi^2 = 38.274$, df = 7, $p < 0.001$, Cramer's $V = 0.265$). The majority of components (COR-E, COR-N, COR-S, COR-W, SAVE2020) display relatively pronounced preferences for spelling word forms with two *l*s instead of one where permissible – an inclination shared with mainly Inner Circle speakers (65% with *ll* vs. 35% with *l*; Peters 2001). COR-UT represents the strongest antithesis to this dominant tendency towards doubled *l* in that alternants with one *l* (66.63%) are preferred over forms with doubled *l* (33.37%). While COR-UT shares this spelling preference with the remaining corpus parts, the preferences evident from COR-C (46% with *ll* vs. 54% with *l*) are not as defined and even weaker for COR-NE (49% with *ll* vs. 51% with *l*). The choices of spelling variants for individual lexical items studied are again markedly varied across the datasets, yielding the same preferences for double *l* forms only for *labelled* as shown in (8) – the remaining items tend to

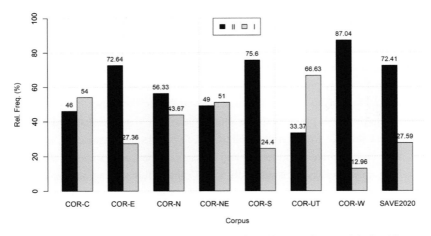

Figure 8 Means of relative frequencies of spelling variants with double or single *l*.

not be spelt similarly across IndEs or do not occur in some corpus components, also inhibiting judgments concerning potential pan-Indian spelling consistencies of the lexical items concerned.

(8) Many a times the youth is <u>labelled</u> as a trouble maker, a no-do-gooder and ends up being imprisoned by drugs or alcohol just to drown his/her frustration. <COR-NE-Meghalaya_Editorial_01.txt>

Fig. 9 depicts preferences concerning the choice of Latinate as opposed to English suffixes. In this regard, the IndEs represented share a preference for Latinate morphological endings – the distribution of Latinate and English suffixes is, in fact, so homogeneous across the corpus components that no significant differences can be attested ($p > 0.05$). Still, only five orthographic alternations were analysed for this spelling-related phenomenon, and the number of corpus examples retained for statistical analysis was relatively low with a total of 108, rendering this analysis less comprehensive than the others presented in Section 4.1. The respective orthographic alternants reveal that Latinate suffixes represent the undisputed choice in COR-C, COR-E, COR-N, COR-S, and SAVE2020, since they do not feature a single English suffix when an alternative Latinate choice was structurally licensed. The only form that occurred with an English suffix and solely accounts for the relative frequencies of English suffixes in COR-NE (4.6%), COR-UT (33.33%), and COR-W (11.11) is *syllabuses* as exemplified in (9), although – for each corpus part other than COR-UT – the preferred spelling of this lexical item is *syllabi* as in

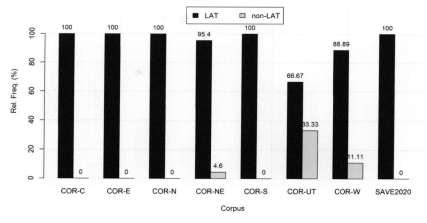

Figure 9 Means of relative frequencies of spelling variants with Latinate suffix absent or present.

(10). The dominant use of Latinate suffixes may paint IndE writing in a conservative light.

(9) Both the central and state governments have announced curtailment of school <u>syllabuses</u>. <COR-W-Goa_NT_Opinion_03.txt>

(10) He also suggested to include a chapter in school text book <u>syllabi</u> on how detainees fought for democracy. <COR-C-Madhya_CC_Bhopal-04.txt>

The contrast between the relative frequencies of abbreviations featuring punctuation as opposed to those that do not is shown for the individual corpus sections in Fig. 10. In line with slight preferences for punctuation omission by mainly Inner Circle speakers (49% with punctuation vs. 51% without; Peters 2001), the IndE corpus components uniformly show preferences for abbreviations without punctuation, although the prominence of these preferences is notably different with only a slight margin for COR-C (48.81% with punctuation vs. 51.19% without), but comparatively large margins for COR-W (14.44% with punctuation vs. 85.56% without) and SAVE2020 (16.59% with punctuation vs. 83.41% without). Rooted in these varying degrees of support for abbreviations without punctuation and the large number of 53,773 corpus examples for the punctuation-related orthographic alternants, said differences across corpus components are statistically significant (χ^2 = 6,191.3, df = 7, p < 0.001, Cramer's V = 0.339). As regards shared spelling preferences in the IndEs studied, *etc.* as in (11) and *ie.* as in (12) habitually feature punctuation while written representations of decades as in (13) or the

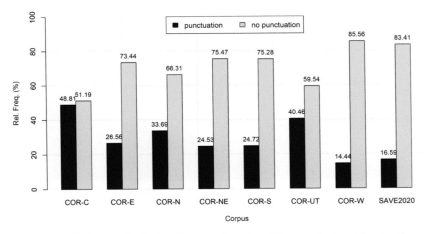

Figure 10 Means of relative frequencies of spelling variants with added or omitted punctuation.

abbreviation for *ante meridiem* as in (14) only rarely do so. Punctuation is also generally absent from realisations of UK and USA in the corpus parts as shown in (15) and (16).

(11) Public Announcement system, chairs, traditional trophies, traditional music etc., were also purchased by Hek at the rate of Rs 41, 10, 000. <COR_NE-Meghalaya_03.txt>

(12) Given that the corporate sector has a no small role in one of the biggest apprehensions about future, i.e. global warming, there needs to be goal-driven and effective steps in that respect. <COR-S-Kerala_Madhyamam_Opinion_03.txt>

(13) While Hindu law overhaul began in the 1950s and continues, activists have long argued that Muslim personal law has remained mostly unchanged. <COR-S-Karnataka_SM_News_05.txt>

(14) The examination started at 11am and concluded at 2pm. <COR-UT-JK_KO_Local_05.txt>

(15) A number of Tagore's plays were performed in London by British and Indian troupes and he was to return to the UK a few more times until 1931. <COR-E-WestBengal_K247-Kolkata_03.txt>

(16) International experts from the USA, Canada, Spain, Germany, Japan, … <COR-N-Uttarakhand_News_Uttarakhand.txt>

In terms of the small set of AmE and BrE spelling pairs (ANALYSE vs. ANALYZE, COLOUR vs. COLOR and GRAY vs GREY), IndE writers – with the exception of ANALYSE in COR-C and COR-UT – markedly prefer BrE over AmE spelling, which may not be surprising given the high status of BrE in the IndE speech community. Still, to offer a more general perspective on how spelling choices evident from the IndE corpus components studied conform with or diverge from one another, the absolute frequencies of occurrence of the individual pairs of orthographic alternations per IndE corpus part are subjected to a cluster analysis. As the widespread k-means cluster analysis requires users to predefine the number of clusters to be established and – in practise – to maybe experiment with different numbers of clusters until the most interpretable groupings have been arrived at, we opted for hierarchical clustering methods since they do not require users to take on the burden of setting a number of clusters to establish and by this potentially bias the outcome and interpretation of the cluster analysis quite fundamentally. Methods of hierarchical cluster analysis fall into the categories of agglomerative and divisive. Agglomerative algorithms start by considering entities as separate and combine most similar entities into a larger cluster – this process is repeated until all entities have been integrated into a single cluster. Divisive hierarchical clustering works the other way round in that it iteratively splits up one large cluster into maximally distinct smaller ones until all entities have been separated from one another.[16] In order to avoid settling for one of the two algorithms and potentially missing important structures in the data, the results of agglomerative and divisive hierarchical clustering of the orthographic IndE data are jointly presented in the tanglegram in Fig. 11. The left part of Fig. 11 shows the clusters produced by agglomerative hierarchical clustering, while the right part of Fig. 11 depicts the results from divisive hierarchical clustering.[17]

The lines across the two dendrograms as well as the clusters coloured in red identify common clusters across both dendrograms, which, from a methodological perspective, profiles the results from both hierarchical agglomerative methods as largely compatible. The only difference across both dendrograms consists in COR-C and COR-UT forming a separate cluster from the remaining corpus sections in the agglomerative dendrogram, while the divisive dendrogram does not profile COR-C and COR-UT as a cluster, but suggests that COR-C is more distinct from the remaining corpus parts than COR-UT. Independent of whether COR-C or COR-UT form a cluster or not, the spelling choices they represent appear to be relatively distinct compared to those of the writers in the remaining corpus parts, mirroring

---

[16] See https://uc-r.github.io/hc_clustering.

[17] Agglomerative hierarchical clustering has been conducted with the *R* package cluster (Maechler et al. 2019) and the tanglegram has been produced with the *R* package dendextend (Galili 2015).

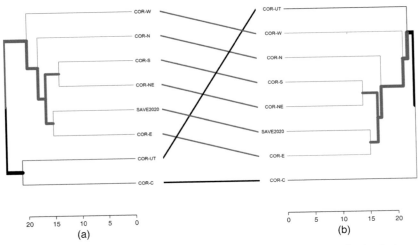

Figure 11 Tanglegram of dendrograms for spelling features devised via hierarchical agglomerative (a) and divisive (b) clustering.

deviations apparent from the frequent omission of *e* (Fig. 6), low frequencies of *l* doubling (Fig. 8), and the comparatively frequent use of punctuation (Fig. 10) with COR-C and from the default omission of *a* (Fig. 5), few instances of *l* doubling (Fig. 8), and the relatively frequent use of English as opposed to Latinate suffixes (Fig. 9) with COR-UT. In contrast, writers featured in the cluster COR-S and COR-NE as well as in the cluster SAVE2020 and COR-E display a large degree of spelling homogeneity. The structure of clusters might thus suggest that a spelling standard has emerged and manifested itself in the newspaper writing of the north-eastern, eastern, and southern parts of India, but that this standard is not (yet) systematically adhered to across the country.

4.2 Multidimensional Analyses of IndEs

From a genre perspective with a focus on 'the culturally expected way of constructing texts' (Biber & Conrad 2019: 16), the individual newspaper texts constituting the IndE corpus parts are organised relatively homogeneously in the sense that a headline (occasionally with a subheader and/or author informa-tion) is followed by paragraphs of texts organised in one or more columns with the occasional picture intervening. Still, from a register perspective, such large degrees of similarity of the IndE texts concerned are less likely. A register analysis rests on three pillars: the situational context, the linguistic structures employed, and their functional relationships (see Biber & Conrad 2019: 6). While their situational contexts of use may still be fairly comparable in that – on a relatively abstract level of communicative purpose – said newspaper texts share the communicative purpose of providing information and opinions on mainly contemporary world affairs, the linguistic features employed may be expected to be subject to more variation across the IndEs covered. Register analyses focus on 'words or grammatical characteristics that are (1) pervasive (distributed throughout a text from the register), and (2) frequent (occurring more commonly in the target register than in most comparison registers)' (Biber & Conrad 2019: 54). In order to complete the third step of a register analysis – establishing the functional relationship between the communicative setting and pervasive linguistic structures – Biber (1989: 3), through Multidimensional Analysis (MDA) by means of a factor analysis of sixty-seven mainly lexical and fewer grammatical features, devised six dimensions 'reflecting underlying shared communicative functions', along which texts and the features they contain can be modelled.[18] The six functional dimensions comprise Dimension 1: involved versus informational production, Dimension 2: narrative versus non-narrative concerns, Dimension 3: explicit versus situation-dependent reference, Dimension 4: overt expression of persuasion, Dimension 5: abstract versus non-abstract information, and Dimension 6: on-line informational elaboration. With the Multidimensional Analysis Tagger (version 1.3; Nini 2019), the IndE corpus sections have been modelled with regard to said six dimensions and the results for dimensions 1 to 3 are visualised in Fig. 12 and for dimensions 4 to 6 in Fig. 16.

Dimension 1 covers a fundamental functional distinction in that texts with higher scores on this dimension tend to 'represent discourse with interactional, affective, involved purposes, associated with strict real-time production and comprehension constraints, versus discourse with highly informational purposes, which is carefully crafted and highly edited' (Biber 1988: 15). With a view to the frequencies of the linguistic features Dimension 1 summarises, the IndE corpus sections display statistically highly significant differences ($\chi^2 = 3{,}553.8$, df $= 182$, $p < 0.001$, Cramer's $V = 0.028$).[19] Among the IndE corpus sections, SAVE2020 is assigned the highest score for Dimension 1, profiling its linguistic structures functionally as the most interactional, affective, and involved among the IndEs studied; in terms of Biber's (1989) prototypical text types, SAVE2020 locates itself between general narrative exposition and scientific exposition, which SAVE2020 approximates, while COR-W sits between scientific and learned

---

[18] Although an MDA analysis aims at offering functional interpretations of linguistic features, these functional interpretations – with the exception of a few truly grammatical categories – largely rest on frequencies of groups of lexical items with similar functions (e.g. time adverbials) or word class frequencies (e.g. attributive or predicative adjectives), which we explore in detail – for this reason we situate this MDA approach in this lexical section.

[19] With the features analysed for Dimension 1, hedges were not considered given their extremely low frequencies in each of the IndE corpus sections studied.

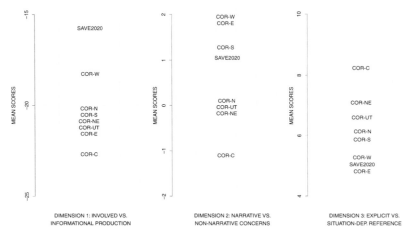

Figure 12 Scores of the IndE corpus components on MDA dimensions 1 to 3.

exposition, the latter being the prototypical text type with the lowest score on Dimension 1. The remaining IndE corpus sections are similar in that the score is even lower than the text type learned exposition and should thus be considered functionally informational, carefully constructed, and highly edited. The association plot in Fig. 13 zooms in on the distribution of the linguistic structures modelled in Dimension 1 by representing expected frequencies of occurrence per corpus section and feature with dashed lines and black/red boxes on top of/below the dashed lines to represent observed frequencies higher/lower than the expected ones, with the relative sizes of the boxes indicating the extents of deviation from the expected frequencies. A noteworthy case in point is NN, namely the overall frequency of nouns, for COR-C in Fig. 13. COR-C has been scored lowest with regard to Dimension 1, which might be – among other linguistic features – rooted in the frequent use of nouns in COR-C as exemplified in (17), which loads negatively on Dimension 1. In contrast, the recurrent occurrence of present-tense verbs (VPRT) as in (18), first-person pronouns (FPP1) as shown in (19), and the use of *not* (XX0) in (20) in COR-W score positively on Dimension 1, since they are used in exchanges characterised by higher degrees of interaction, affection, and involvement.[20]

(17) College of NSS program officer Dr. Dharmendra Bahadur Singh said that NSS achievers of 20 colleges were present for the program, with the objective of removing the deficiencies in the NSS order and strengthening the country by

---

[20] For the deviations from expected values for XX0, consider the last set of bars to the right in the association plot in Fig. 13. The feature label XX0 has been suppressed due to lack of plotting space.

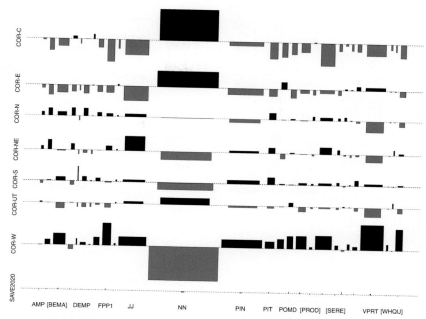

Figure 13 Association plot of features for MDA Dimension 1.

strengthening by making a strong <u>National</u> <u>Service</u> <u>Scheme</u>. <COR-C-Madhya_CC_Bhopal-01.txt>[21]

(18) MMC <u>has</u> been asked to make use of the two identified sites for the purpose of storing the end product and that it <u>is</u> the GWMC's duty to cover the RDF that <u>is</u> stored. <COR-W-Goa_NT_GoaNews01.txt>

(19) '[...] Considering it, <u>we</u> have demanded a package for the Dairy from the government and if <u>we</u> get it <u>we</u> can rollback the price hike,' administrator Arvind Kutkar said, while addressing media. <COR-W-Goa_NT_GoaNews_01.txt>

(20) Addressing a press conference at the state secretariat, Sawaikar urged such Goans <u>not</u> to worry as the particular act would <u>not</u> have any impact on them. <COR-W-Goa_NT_GoaNews_01.txt>

Dimension 2 describes the extent to which texts display concern for narration – also with regard to this dimension, statistically significant differences exist across the IndE corpus components (χ^2 = 1,223.3, df = 49, $p < 0.001$, Cramer's $V = 0.031$), although most of them share that they are located between

---

[21] In examples (17) to (20), the relevant forms counted in the MDA analysis are underlined disregarding potential tagging errors.

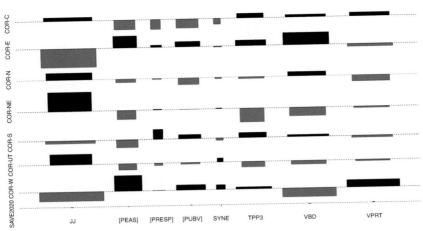

Figure 14 Association plot of features for MDA Dimension 2.

Biber's (1988) text types general narrative exposition and informational inter-action. COR-C is an exception in that its score is notably lower compared to other sections and is more readily comparable to structures to be found in intimate interpersonal interaction, while COR-E and particularly COR-W rank higher for narrative concern and display slightly higher scores than the text type general narrative concern on this dimension. Looking at the distribution of individual structural features, the association plot for Dimension 2 in Fig. 14 indicates that adjective use (JJ), which is considered rather non-narrative than narrative (see Biber 1989: 8), figures particularly prominently in COR-NE as exemplified in (21). In contrast, perfect-aspect verbs (PEAS) and past-tense verbs (VBD) are two structures characteristic of narrative concern, with the former occurring with remarkable frequency in COR-W as in (22) and the latter in COR-E as in (23).

(21) The objective of Act East Policy is to promote <u>economic</u> cooperation, <u>cultural</u> ties and develop <u>strategic</u> relationship with countries in the Asia-Pacific region through <u>continuous</u> engagement at <u>bilateral</u>, <u>regional</u> and <u>multilateral</u> levels thereby providing <u>enhanced</u> connectivity to the North East including Arunachal Pradesh with <u>other</u> <u>neighbouring</u> countries. <COR-NE-Arunachal_ArunachalTimes_Editorials_01.txt>

(22) However, the fee hike <u>has put</u> a stop to unnecessary purchase of forms by the applicants which <u>has helped</u> the department to save money on printing cost and also provides revenue. <COR-W-Goa_NT_GoaNews_01.txt>

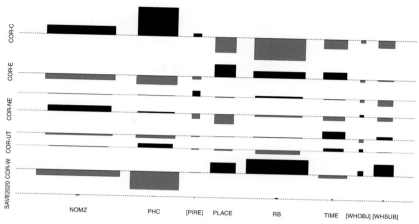

Figure 15 Association plot of features for MDA Dimension 3.

(23) The IIC <u>said</u> Jhunjhunwala <u>said</u> he <u>was</u> sorry but also <u>said</u> it <u>was</u> a mistake.
<COR-E-Odisha_2015_01.txt>

Biber (1988: 148) provides the following description of the discriminatory power of Dimension 3 (illustrated in the association plot in Fig. 15): '[T]his dimension distinguishes between informational texts that mark referents in an elaborated and explicit manner, and situated texts that depend on direct reference to, or extensive knowledge of, the physical and temporal situation of discourse production for understanding.' Although all of the IndE corpus components rank higher in terms of their contextual explicitness than the most explicit text type learned exposition according to Biber (1989), it is the extent to which the individual IndE corpus components are more explicit than learned exposition that triggers the statistically highly significant differences (χ^2 = 810.86, df = 49, p < 0.001, Cramer's V = 0.039). COR-C is the IndE corpus component where the context is most elaborated, while COR-W, SAVE2020, and COR-E display lower degrees of contextual explicitness. Phrasal coordination (PHC) is one of the indicators of structural explicitness, which occurs with noteworthy frequency in COR-C as shown in (24). Conversely, overall adverb use (RB), regarded as a marker of situation-dependent discourse, is particularly high in COR-W (as in (25)) and place adverbials (PLACE), which also instantiate discursive non-explicitness, occur comparatively often in COR-E as evident from (26).

(24) During the next 24 hours, Active Monsoon conditions are likely over parts of Jammu <u>and</u> Kashmir, Himachal Pradesh <u>and</u> Uttarakhand, few places of Punjab, Haryana <u>and</u> Northeast Rajasthan along with Delhi, West Uttar Pradesh,

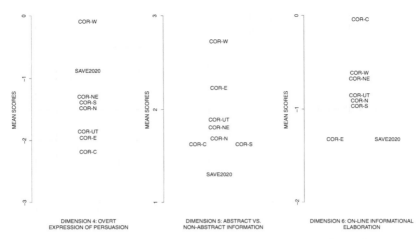

Figure 16 Scores of the IndE corpus components on MDA dimensions 4 to 6.

South Konkan, and Goa, Coastal Karnataka, and Coastal Andhra Pradesh. <COR-C-Madhya_CC_Bhopal-01.txt>

(25) 'But the government is not granting permission for sand extraction and, hence, traditional sand extractors are either forced to undertake sand extraction illegally or completely give up.' <COR-W-Goa_NT_GoaNews_01.txt>

(26) Some prominent publishers from across the country have put up their stalls selling books of all genres from across the world, and are offering attractive discounts. <COR-E-Odisha_2015_01.txt>

Dimension 4 organises texts on a cline from non-persuasive to persuasive texts. Most IndE corpus components are grouped between the relatively non-persuasive text types general narrative exposition and scientific exposition, with the latter being more non-persuasive than the former. Still, also with Dimension 4 significant differences across the IndE corpus components exist (χ^2 = 445.88, df = 42, p < 0.001, Cramer's V = 0.046) – COR-C is profiled as the least persuasive IndE corpus component with a lower score than scientific exposition, whereas SAVE2020 and COR-W display the highest Dimension 4 measures among the IndE corpus sections, ranking higher than general narrative exposition. With regard to strongest deviations of individual Dimension 4 features from expected frequencies, necessity modals (NEMD) such as *ought*, *should*, or *must* exemplified in (27) as well as predictive modals (PRMD) like *will*, *would*, or *shall* in (28) are encountered frequently in COR-C. Although necessity and predictive modals are considered indicators of overt expression of persuasion and they are especially frequent in COR-C compared to other IndE corpus sections, the remaining structural features indicating the persuasive nature of texts occur systematically less frequently than expected in COR-C, characterising this corpus part as the least persuasive among the ones studied.

(27) Expressing concern over the quality of construction works, he said that for the works which have been delayed due to the wrong design of the consultant, the accountability of the consultant <u>should</u> be fixed, recoveries <u>should</u> be made from them and they <u>should</u> be blacklisted. <COR-C-Madhya_CC_Bhopal-01. txt>

(28) Streamlining and rationalizing the approvals <u>would</u> promote ease of doing business in the sector, attracting new investment which <u>would</u> give a boost to the sector. <COR-C-Madhya_CC_Bhopal-01.txt>

With regard to the question to what degree texts portray abstract versus non-abstract information, 'genres have high values on Dimension 5 to the extent that they focus on abstract, conceptual or technical subject matter' (Biber 1988: 154). While the majority of text ranks between learned exposition and general narrative exposition with a clear orientation towards learned exposition, COR-E and COR-W deviate from this grouping in that their structural features portray higher degrees of abstractness than learned exposition – a tendency particularly pronounced with COR-W. Again, the differences between the individual IndE corpus components are statistically highly significant ($\chi^2 = 240.72$, df $= 35$, $p < 0.001$, Cramer's $V = 0.045$) and the most notable deviations from expected frequencies of occurrence can be attested for the use of *by*-passives (BYPA), a marker of abstract discourse, in COR-N as in (29) and COR-NE (30), although the two IndE corpus sections are not particularly abstract across all the features relevant for Dimension 5.

(29) The move came at a meeting of the state disaster management authority (SDMA) <u>chaired by</u> Lieutenant-Governor Anil Baijal and <u>was attended by</u> Vice-Chairperson Chief Minister Arvind Kejriwal, among others. <COR-N-NCTDelhi_NCRDelhi_01–54.txt>

(30) The strong campaign <u>run by</u> Congress and more number of seats <u>won by</u> it, in compare to previous election shows that BJP is vulnerable. <COR-NE-Arunachal_ArunachalTimes_Editorials_01.txt>

High scores on Dimension 6 indicate texts of an informational nature that have been created under certain production pressure. As a documentation of how the individual structural features load on this dimension is not available in Biber (1989), we offer only the fairly general points that (a) there is again a group of IndE corpus sections that display relatively similar scores and (b)

COR-C ranks notably higher and SAVE2020 and COR-E rank notably lower than the remaining IndE corpus parts.

From a bird's-eye perspective, two groups of IndE corpus sections analysed emerge, namely one group of IndE corpus components that are habitually placed around the extreme higher and lower MDA scores attested for the IndE newspaper texts analysed and another group of IndE corpus texts that tends to occupy the middle ground between said extreme MDA scores, which is the case for COR-N, COR-NE, COR-S, and COR-UT. Consequently, these IndE corpus sections are profiled as relatively unmarked with regard to any of the MDA register features analysed compared to other IndE newspaper texts. This is different for the remaining corpus sections. Texts in COR-C combine informational production with non-narrative concern, explicit reference without overt expression of persuasion and on-line informational elaboration, profiling said IndE corpus section as a fact-oriented collection of texts that does not seek to actively engage with or manipulate its audience. This makes COR-C stand out from the remaining corpus sections in the sense that no other IndE corpus component shares any of said register features to the extremes with which they are present in COR-C. From an MDA-based register perspective, COR-C contrasts sharply with COR-W as well as SAVE2020 in that their texts generally portray involved production and situation-dependent reference – with COR-W differentiating itself from SAVE2020 by also displaying narrative concern, overt expression of persuasion, and abstract information in its texts, while SAVE2020 is characterised by non-abstract information and a lack of on-line informational elaboration. COR-E also tends to fall into this generally more speech-like and less formal group of IndE corpus sections in that its texts show narrative concern and context dependence, but – like SAVE2020 – a lack of production pressure.

In the light of the two overall groups of IndE texts, namely one the MDA profiles as relatively unmarked with regard to the MDA dimensions in comparison to other IndE newspaper texts and another that allows devising the distinctive MDA profiles just outlined, the clusters evident from the tanglegram in Fig. 17 are not surprising. The IndE corpus sections that produced relatively average scores across all MDA dimensions, namely COR-N, COR-NE, COR-S, and COR-UT, form two clusters that are joined before the remaining IndE corpus sections are combined with them – the first one being COR-W as one of the more informal, speech-like IndE corpus components. The other two informal, speech-like IndE corpus sections COR-E and SAVE2020 are joined with the aforementioned cluster with the order in which they are joined being influenced by whether or not agglomerative or divisive hierarchical clustering has been conducted. Still, the more qualitative descriptions of the MDA scores

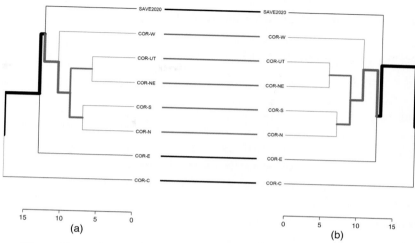

Figure 17 Tanglegram of dendrograms for MDA features devised via hierarchical agglomerative (a) and divisive (b) clustering.

of these individual IndE corpus sections revealed this group of corpus texts as conceptually relatively homogeneous, but markedly distinct from the formal and conceptually more written nature of the texts in COR-C, which is represented in the fact that COR-C is most removed from the cluster of texts of the remaining IndE corpus sections.

In comparison to the tanglegram for spelling features in Fig. 11, certain parallels become apparent in the cluster structure of the MDA tanglegram. COR-C is represented as distinct from other IndE newspaper texts in both tanglegrams – maybe with the exception that, in the hierarchical agglomerative clustering for spelling, COR-C together with COR-UT forms a cluster different from the remaining corpus parts. COR-S and COR-NE are also grouped in relatively compatible ways across the spelling and the MDA tanglegram. Both IndE corpus sections constitute a cluster in the spelling tanglegram and, although both components do not form a cluster in the MDA tanglegram on their own, the clusters they are part of are joined to a cluster on the next hierarchical level. COR-W in terms of spelling and MDA features and COR-N with regard to spelling share that they are located between the more homogenous and more distinct IndE corpus sections. In terms of notable differences across the spelling and MDA tanglegrams, SAVE2020, whose spelling conventions appear relatively compatible with a number of other IndE newspaper texts such as COR-NE and COR-S, but particularly COR-E, differentiates itself more markedly with its MDA scores. COR-E also stands out more clearly from an MDA perspective compared to

the spelling clusters. The MDA scores of COR-UT group this corpus component with other IndE corpus sections, although COR-UT displayed rather
specific spelling preferences.

4.3 Lexical Innovation in IndEs

Although newspapers can certainly not be regarded as cradles of linguistic
innovation in comparison to other communicative settings like informal face-
to-face conversations or linguistic exchanges on social media platforms, they
nevertheless serve as a salient means to judge the degree of general acceptance
and standardisation of novel lexemes in varieties where other means of codifi-
cation are absent and – in case so far unrecorded word forms do in fact occur in
newspapers – they are most probably already firmly established in the variety
concerned. Against this background, CORINNE and the Indian component of
SAVE2020 have also been investigated for hitherto unrecorded lexemes. The
analysis proceeded as outlined here:

1. From CORINNE and the Indian component of SAVE2020, a word list of all
   forms featured in the respective corpus components was created.
2. Each word form retrieved from the corpus was checked in the online version
   of the OED (OED Online 2022) to establish whether the word form concerned had already been documented in the OED. While, unsurprisingly, an
   overwhelming amount of word forms from the IndE datasets is covered in
   the OED, 17,357 words are not. Still, given that the OED does not feature
   proper names and a certain selection of transparent word-formations (e.g.
   non-agriculture or *non-creamy* from the IndE dataset were not found in the
   OED), only a subset of word forms not part of the OED word stock merits
   further investigation.
3. In addition to discarding proper names, the 17,357 unrecorded forms were
   searched for derivational affixes as indicators of potentially newly formed
   (hybrid) lexemes.[22] The IndE forms left were checked against (a) the
   American and British components of the *News on the Web* corpus (NOW;
   Davies 2016–) to make sure that these forms are not part of the common core
   of English and (b) two reference works for the lexis of IndE, namely the
   Handbook of Usage and Pronunciation (Nihalani et al. 2004) and
   A Dictionary of Indian English (Carls 2017).

---

[22] The derivational prefixes and suffixes listed in Plag (2003) were used to search the list of IndE
forms not recorded in the OED. Prefixes considered were *a-, an-, anti-, de-, dis-, in-, mis-, non-,*
and *un-*. The suffixes included *-able, -age, -al, -an-, -ance, -ancy, -ant, -ary, -ate, -ce, -cy, -dom, -
ean, -ed, -ee, -eer, -en, -ence, -ency, -er, -ery, -esque, -ess, -ful, -ful, -hood, -ian, -ible, -ic, -ical, -
ify, -ing, -ing, -ion, -ise, -ish, -ism, -ist, -ity, -ive, -ize, -less, -ly, -ly, -ment, -ness, -or, -ous, -ry,* and
-ship.

While producing ample evidence of already recorded IndE forms such as the verbal LATHICHARGE, namely hitting someone with a long stick, or the verb GHERAO, namely protesting/demonstrating against something or someone, along the way this procedure profiled five so far unrecorded IndE lexemes: CRACKERLESS (adj.), IMPLEADMENT (n.), SAFFRONISATION (n.), SAFFRONISE (v.), and TELECALLER (n.).

In BrE CRACKER generally refers to 'a gift, perhaps a small trinket or novelty of some kind, which pops when pulled sharply from each end' (Nihalani et al. 2004: 58–59). Contrastively, the IndE nominal use of CRACKER as a shortening of the more complex FIRECRACKER stands for a small and generally controllable explosive usually used in the context of celebrations to make loud noise without the benefit of an enclosed gift. The so far unrecorded derived adjective CRACKERLESS stands for celebrations without said loud explosives as illustrated in (31) and (32) with reference to the customs during Diwali, the Festival of Lights.

(31) SC refuses to change its stand on 'cracker-less diwali', hurt by communal angle <COR-N-NCTDelhi_NCRDelhi_301–400.txt>

(32) 'Every year, animal shelters witness a tremendous increase in the number of runaway and lost pets, who are scared, anxious, nervous and often burnt. That's why we are all for a cracker-less Diwali', says Sally. <SAVE2020–IND_ToI_4514949.txt>

In the OED, the verb IMPLEAD is defined as suing someone/something in a court of justice. The undocumented derived noun IMPLEADMENT is – as evident from examples (33) to (34) – the process of taking someone/something to court.

(33) The Supreme Court has adjourned to September 9 hearing into the inter-locutory application filed by some village panchayats from the mining belt seeking impleadment in the Goa mining case. <COR-W-Goa_NT_GoaNews_08.txt>

(34) Filing an impleadment application, Mr. Chaudhary claimed that Mr. Tuseed did not disclose to DU authorities that an FIR was lodged against him . . .. <COR-N-NCTDelhi_NCRDelhi_301–400.txt>

Although a Wikipedia entry for the noun SAFFRONISATION exists,[23] this nominal form and the related verb SAFFRONISE have so far not been

---

[23] The Wikipedia page for SAFFRONISATION can be viewed at https://en.wikipedia.org/wiki/Saffronisation (last accessed 18 November 2022).

documented in the OED or the two IndE reference works considered. These novel forms are also absent from American and British newspaper texts in NOW. SAFFRONISE as in (35) stands for implementing that kind of Hindu nationalist agendas usually located on the right wing of the political spectrum and SAFFRONISATION as in (36) signifies said process. The lack of earlier documentation of these lexemes might be related to Bhatia's (2020) observation that Indian nationalist currents have grown stronger and thus have become more readily perceivable only comparatively recently, implying that Nihalani et al. (2004) and Carls (2017) may have been published too early to capture these lexemes, since the concepts they evoke might not have been as present or as societally relevant and debated as they currently are.

(35) He expressed concern that the NDA government was trying to include communal elements and <u>saffronise</u> education in India. <COR-S-Andhra_HI_ Andhra_07.txt>

(36) It however comes as a great letdown that an assortment of leaders who were once the staunchest critics of the BJP is today wholeheartedly aiding in the <u>saffronisation</u> of the entire nation. <COR-W-Goa_NT_Opinion_01.txt>

The noun TELECALLER shown in (37) stands for someone working in a call centre to conduct business with prospective or existing clients of a particular company.

(37) Saurabh, who has studied till Class 12, worked as a <u>telecaller</u> at HDFC life insurance's call centre. <COR-W-Gujarat_AM_News_Crime_01.txt>

Fig. 18 provides the normalised frequencies per million words (pmw) of these so far undocumented lexemes in the IndE corpus components. Given the relative novelty of the lexemes as well as the genre(s) of newspaper texts in which they are found, it is not unexpected that the lexemes concerned occur rarely – in fact, only SAFFRONISATION and SAFFRONISE occur more than once in a million words in COR-E, while all the other forms are less frequent across all corpus components studied. In terms of the dispersion of the lexemes discussed, CRACKERLESS is attested only (once respectively) in COR-NE and SAVE2020, while SAFFRONISE and SAFFRONISATION occur across five of the eight IndE corpus components studied.

In line with findings from spelling in Section 4.1 and MDA in Section 4.2, COR-C stands out from the remaining corpus components again in that it is the only component not featuring any of the undocumented lexemes discussed. COR-S and COR-NE cannot be considered hotbeds for linguistic innovation in that only relatively few innovations can be encountered in these two corpus

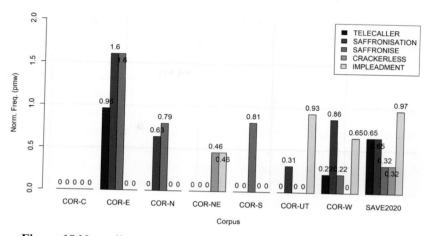

Figure 18 Normalised frequencies (pmw) of so far undocumented IndE lexemes.

components. Said similarities across both corpus components are also in line with the observation that they formed a cluster based on the spelling analyses as shown in Fig. 11 and the MDA cluster analyses also highlighted their similarities. COR-W featuring four out of five innovative lexemes and SAVE2020, in which all novel forms have been attested, appear more receptive to lexical linguistic innovations, considering the admittedly small amount of lexemes studied. In the tanglegram of the MDA analyses in Fig. 17, COR-W and SAVE2020 were also notably separated from the remaining – a tendency which apparently continues with the lexical innovations at hand.

5 Morphosyntax

Following the studies of lexical variation in the previous section, we analyse morphosyntactic variation in CORINNE and SAVE2020 in Section 5. First, we consider mass and count nouns in Section 5.1. Then, we move on to *only* and *itself* as focus markers in Section 5.2 before considering combinations of verb + *about* in Section 5.3. Finally, in the last case study of this Element, we provide an analysis of 'intrusive *as*' in Section 5.4.

5.1 Mass and Count Nouns

Some languages, such as English, make a distinction between mass nouns and count nouns. The latter type refers to items that can be quantified and which have a morphologically marked plural form. Mass nouns, on the other hand, have an inherently singular form which is not marked for number, although they may be modified by quantifiers such as *some* (Schmidtke & Kuperman 2017: 136–7). While a well-documented tendency exists among speakers of Inner Circle varieties to blur the boundaries between mass and count nouns in some contexts (e.g. by using the determiner *less* with countable nouns instead of the more standard *fewer*, as in *less students*) (Tallerman 2020: 10), it is this variability along the mass-count divide which is considered to be 'a discernible linguistic marker of the boundary between native and non-native varieties of English' (see McArthur 2002; Mesthrie & Bhatt 2008, quoted in Schmidtke & Kuperman 2017: 136). What is more, according to Sedlatschek (2009: 227–8), this variability 'has been claimed to be a peculiarity of the IndE noun phrase' and can be said to encompass the treatment of non-count nouns as count nouns, the introduction of morphological number contrast for unmarked plurals, use of plural nouns in the singular, as well as the treatment of singular nouns as variable nouns. From the range of mass-count noun variability outlined by Sedlatschek (2009), the following analysis focuses on the first sub-variant, namely the treatment of mass nouns as count nouns. This can safely be described as a characteristic feature of IndE. For example, the *electronic World Atlas of Varieties of English* (eWAVE, Kortmann et al. 2020) places IndE in Category A regarding the feature 'Different count/mass noun distinctions resulting in use of plural for StE singular', meaning that this feature is considered 'pervasive or obligatory' in the variety.[24]

Sedlatschek's (2009: 229) quantitative corpus analysis of mass/count nouns in IndE led him to conclude that, since the token frequencies of the non-standard uses are lower than those of the standard uses in the *Kolhapur Corpus*, 'contemporary IndE largely follows the codified conventions'. Nevertheless, data from the 2000 Primary Corpus gathered by Sedlatschek suggests that English-language Indian press was becoming more open towards non-standard mass/count noun uses over time.[25] With data from the CORINNE and SAVE2020 corpora originating fifteen to twenty years later than the data in the Primary Corpus, it is reasonable to suspect that we should find even more examples of nouns displaying non-standard variation along the count/non-count divide in both SAVE2020 and CORINNE. Consistent with our previous predictions and findings that the data from CORINNE contains more examples of non-standard language use than SAVE2020 due to its regional nature, we predict that the same should hold for the pluralisation of mass nouns.

---

[24] The relevant entry can be found at https://ewave-atlas.org/languages/52.

[25] A 180,000-word corpus of spoken and written IndE, comprised of the genres press, broadcast, and student essays (Sedlatschek 2009: 41).

As the basis for our noun selection, we began with the list of the 25 'truly uncountable' nouns used by Hall et al. (2013) for their study of noun pluralisation in world Englishes, excluding nine items from the list which, to the best of our knowledge, have not been attested as count nouns in IndE thus far. To this list, we added six more mass nouns which were found to frequently be pluralised in world Englishes by Schmidtke and Kuperman (2017: 139), as well as five additional nouns which, according to Sedlatschek (2009: 243), regularly show the properties of count nouns in contemporary IndE. This gave us a total of 28 nouns.[26] The data extraction procedure was conducted using *AntConc* (Anthony 2022). For each of the nouns on our list, we separately queried each regional sub-corpus of CORINNE (C, E, N, NCT, NE, S, W, UT-AN, and UT-JK) as well as the IndE component of the SAVE2020 corpus for the following cases: the plural form of the noun (e.g. *machineries*), the singular form preceded directly by the indefinite article *a/an* (e.g. *a machinery*), as well as the singular noun and the indefinite articles *a/an* separated by one up to three words, in order to capture such cases as *a proper administrative machinery*. For each item, all identified uses of it as a countable noun were then added together. Finally, for each sub-corpus, the absolute frequencies of the 28 nouns were added together, a normalised pttw (per ten thousand words) frequency was computed, and the top items were identified. Tables 5 and 6 summarise the results.

Comparing the results obtained for CORINNE and SAVE2020, we can see that the items on our list of typically uncountable nouns are found nearly twice as often in the form of count nouns in CORINNE compared to SAVE2020 (0.92 pttw vs. 0.5 pttw), likely due to CORINNE's more regional nature. These results are statistically significant according to the Wilcoxon Signed-Rank Test, which tests for a difference between the means of two not normally distributed populations (Levshina 2015: 87) ($n = 28$, $W = 49$, lower than the critical value of $W = 82$ at the $p = 0.005$ level). Conducting a chi-square test on the numbers of countable and non-countable instances of the nouns also yields significant results ($\chi^2 = 12.762$, df $= 1$, $p < 0.001$, Cramer's $V = 0.011$). Based on the top ten most frequent countable nouns list, the two corpora have the following items in common: *agitation, evidence, legislation, infrastructure,* and *aircraft*.

Inspecting the results for the individual sub-components of CORINNE, it becomes clear how much diversity is actually present in IndE when it comes to

---

[26] The full list is *advice, applause, baggage, cash, corruption, employment, equipment, evidence, information, jewellery, knowledge, luggage, slang, software, traffic, violence* (from Hall et al. 2013) + *awareness, education, infrastructure, migration, entertainment, training* (from Schmidtke & Kuperman 2017) + *legislation, agitation, machinery, aircraft, tuition* (from Sedlatschek 2009). Excluded were the nouns *dew, fun, furniture, hardware, homework, luck, money, music, underwear* (from Hall et al. 2013).

Table 5 Frequencies of countable and non-countable
nouns in CORINNE and SAVE2020.

Corpus	CORINNE	SAVE2020
Countable	2,537	154
Countable pttw	0.92	0.5
Non-countable	93,860	7,702
Total	96,397	7,856
% Count./Total	2.63%	1.96%

the usage frequency of the countable mass nouns on our list. The regions West, UT-JK, and the North have the fewest instances of the nouns under investigation (with 0.58 pttw, 0.61 pttw, and 0.62 pttw, respectively), while the regions North-East (1.34 pttw) and UT-AN (1.65 pttw) tend to use them the most frequently, surpassing the average for the entire CORINNE corpus. These results can also be considered highly statistically significant ($\chi^2 = 110.72$, df = 8, $p < 0.001$, Cramer's $V = 0.034$). *Agitation* (38) appears to be the most prevalent countable mass noun, being among the top five items for each sub-corpus under investigation (except for COR-UT-AN) and making up 20.3% of the 2691 total instances of countable mass nouns identified in the entire data. This is followed by *equipment* (11.3%) (39), *training* (9.1%) (40), *aircraft* (8.2%), and *evidence* (8.1%) (41) (see Table 7 for a summary).

(38) Instead of focusing on any of these issues the Congress wants to launch an agitation against a movie?! <COR-W-Maharashtra_BridgeChronicle_Opinion. txt>

(39) Those living in the rural areas also don't have enough beds and also short of COVID medical teams and equipments such as ventilators etc. <COR-NE-Nagaland_NP_Editorial_01.txt>

(40) resource persons from mainland shall be invited to impart trainings on design improvement, garment and fashion designing <COR-UT-AN_AS_City_12.txt>

(41) 'The police have got lot of evidence to corroborate this information, but we are still waiting for a conclusive evidence to come to our knowledge,' he said. <SAVE2020_TS_4627072.txt>

The least-attested (but not entirely unrepresented) nouns from the list are *slang* (0.1%) (42), *luggage* (0.4%), *entertainment* (0.4%), *violence* (0.5%) (43), and *employment* (0.5%) (44). Due to their low frequency these cases may, of

Table 6 Frequencies of countable and non-countable nouns in the CORINNE sub-corpora.

Sub-Corpus	C	E	N	NCT	NE	S	W	UT AN	UT JK
Count.	74	245	94	61	845	585	270	264	99
Count. pttw	1.01	0.79	0.62	0.89	1.34	0.79	0.58	1.65	0.61
Non-count.	3,209	8,167	5,423	2,254	24,802	24,866	12,354	7,856	4,929
Total	3,283	8,412	5,517	2,315	25,647	25,451	12,624	8,120	5,028
% Count./Total	2.25%	2.91%	1.7%	2.63%	3.3%	2.3%	2.14%	3.25%	1.97%

course, represent accidental misspellings or examples of idiosyncratic innovations. They may also, however, be newly emerging variants.

(42) Sayings, proverbs, idioms and even <u>slangs</u> may be in different languages, but we can learn from the knowledgeable persons that the message in each of them bear similarity for the most part. <COR-S-Karnataka_SM_Editorial_01.txt>

(43) Campaigning for the second phase saw <u>a bloody violence</u> when two unidentified assailants shot dead BJP leader from Khurda Manguli Jena April 14 night. <COR-E-Odisha_2019_01.txt>

(44) Women are focused on their <u>employments</u> and appreciate positions of responsibility <COR-UT-JK_KO_InDepth_01.txt>

A surprising discovery is the (very infrequent, but not unattested with 0.7% of all instances) usage of *cash* (45–47) as a count noun, which was identified in five of CORINNE's nine sub-corpora (NCT, NE, S, W, and UT-AN). The most countable uses of *cash* were found in the COR-NCT-Delhi and the COR-NE components (with a normalised frequency of 0.04 pttw and 0.02 pttw, respectively). Another surprising item on the list which has, to our knowledge, not yet been discussed as a count noun in IndE is *applause* (48), making up 0.8% of all instances and appearing in all (sub-) corpora, except for COR-NE and COR-W.

(45) the police detected one kilogram of gold and <u>a hard cash</u> of Rs.88.22 lakhs. <COR-S-Andhra_HI_02.txt>

Table 7 Ten most frequent countable mass nouns in CORINNE and SAVE2020.

	CORINNE	Frequency (pttw)	SAVE2020	Frequency (pttw)
1	*agitation*	468 (0.17)	*aircraft*	60 (0.19)
2	*equipment*	277 (0.10)	*agitation*	29 (0.09)
3	*training*	230 (0.08)	*legislation*	12 (0.04)
4	*evidence*	181 (0.07)	*evidence*	7 (0.02)
5	*legislation*	166 (0.06)	*infrastructure*	5 (0.02)
6	*infrastructure*	151 (0.05)	*advice*	4 (0.01)
7	*aircraft*	141 (0.05)	*equipment*	4 (0.01)
8	*machinery*	126 (0.05)	*software*	4 (0.01)
9	*information*	78 (0.03)	*applause*	3 (0.01)
10	*education*	49 (0.02)	*awareness*	3 (0.01)

(46) Huge amounts of <u>cashes</u> were also seized from different parts of the state though it has not been linked to any political party as of now. <COR-NE-Meghalaya_03.txt>

(47) The award consists of <u>a cash</u> of Rs 15,000, a citation, a seleng sador and a bundle of books. <NE-Assam_State_2015–12.txt>

(48) Students later gave him <u>a thunderous applause</u> for his speech. <COR-S_Kerala_Madhyamam_04.txt

The five most frequent countable mass nouns per CORINNE sub-corpus are as follows:

- COR-C: *equipment, evidence, training, agitation, aircraft*
- COR-E: *agitation, evidence, equipment, jewellery, aircraft*
- COR-N: *agitation, legislation, education, knowledge, training*
- COR-NCT: *aircraft, evidence, agitation, equipment, feedback*
- COR-NE: *training, infrastructure, equipment, agitation, machinery*
- COR-S: *agitation, legislation, evidence, aircraft, training, equipment*
- COR-W: *agitation, aircraft, evidence, legislation, tuition*
- COR-UT-AN: *equipment, training, information, aircraft, machinery*
- COR-UT-JK: *evidence, equipment, agitation, aircraft, education*

In accordance with our initial predictions, CORINNE does appear to contain more cases of countable mass nouns than SAVE2020, at least with respect to the 28 'truly uncountable' nouns from our list. The difference, however, cannot yet be considered statistically significant. Nonetheless, the wide range of results obtained for CORINNE's individual sub-corpora offers us a glimpse into the diversity present in IndEs, with the normalised frequencies ranging anywhere from 0.58 pttw (for COR-W) to 1.65 pttw (for COR-UT-AN). The high prevalence of such mass nouns as *equipment, evidence, training, aircraft*, and others in a countable form is not surprising, as they have already been attested in previous studies. Arguably more intriguing is the presence of such traditionally uncountable nouns as *violence, cash, applause, slang*, and *employment* in the corpora, despite their low frequencies, which may indicate their transition to a countable form in (some of) the IndEs. Thus, we suggest that close attention should be paid to them in future studies.

5.2 Focus Markers *Only* and *Itself*

One of the standard functions of *only* is as an exclusive or restrictive focus particle, that is, limiting the meaning of a lexical item by excluding further alternatives from consideration (Lange 2007: 183). Numerous studies of the use of the focus marker *only* in IndEs have attested to the existence of a 'presentational' or emphasising function of the focus marker in addition to the contrastive function present in other English varieties (e.g. Mesthrie 1992; Bhatt 2000; Bhatt 2004; Lange 2007; Mesthrie & Bhatt 2008; Sedlatschek 2009: 300). What is more, there is sufficient evidence to consider it 'a phenomenon that is the exclusive property of New Indian Englishes' (Lange 2007: 182).

Fig. 19 as well as examples (49–51) illustrate presentational *only*. A token of *only* was categorised as presentational if the context did not allow a contrastive reading. If *only* were an exclusive focus marker in (51), then we would expect a contrast or an implicit alternative to 'this democracy *only* [and not some other democracy]'. However, the whole news story is solely concerned with political affairs in West Bengal; no other democracy is mentioned so that a contrastive reading is ruled out. Similarly, the sign in Fig. 19 'please leave your footwear outside *only*' would be rather odd in a contrastive reading: 'leave your footwear *only* outside [not anywhere else]'. *Only* in this context is much more likely to be presentational, putting particular emphasis on the request to leave footwear outside, please.

(49) In this lefter [*sic*; 'letter'] only, the SMS evidence shows that the meeting date was mentioned as end of February. <COR-W-Maharashtra_Lokmat_ News.txt>

(50) the government of Italy has asked the Italian nationals to stay in India only, for the time being <SAVE2020_TS_4624643.txt>

(51) This journey is being done to save this democracy only. <COR-E-WestBengal_K247_Westbengal_06.txt>

Another innovative focus marker that has been attested in IndE is *itself* (see Lange 2007; Lange 2012; and (52) to (54)), which has also developed a presentational function, and which can be employed in IndE as an alternative to presentational *only*. *Itself* can occur not only after noun phrases, as in other varieties of English, but also following adverbials (e.g. *from on itself*, quoted in Lange 2012: 186). There is again enough evidence to suggest that the use of *itself* as a presentational focus marker may be approaching grammaticalisation. Frequently, uses of *itself* display a lack of agreement with the focus, which means that it may be becoming an invariant particle (Lange 2012: 186). For discussions on the possible reasons for the emergence of these innovative uses of *only* and *itself* as presentational focus markers, see Lange (2007) and (2012).

Figure 19 Example of focus marker *only* (picture taken by Claudia Lange in Shilparamam, Hyderabad, in 2019).

(52) Such a thoughtful approach on the part of government would be able to nip the future disorder in the bud <u>itself</u>. <COR-S-Telangana_TT_Opinion_01.txt>

(53) In times as such, when humans <u>itself</u> becomes the agents of risks making our society a risk society <COR-NE-Nagaland_ME_Editorial_01.txt>

(54) Even now, a large number of shopkeepers are closing their shops around 4 p.m., <u>itself</u> <COR-N-Uttarakhand_News_Dehradun_01.txt>

Lange's (2012) contrastive study of the uses of *only* and *itself* in ICE-India and ICE-Great Britain (ICE-GB) has provided evidence that both particles are not only more frequent in IndE than in BrE (with *itself* occurring as much as seven times more frequently in the IndE data), but presentational functions of both are completely absent from ICE-GB. However, even among IndEs, there is variation in usage frequency. Lange's (2007) study of *only* and *itself* showed that presentational *only* is very common in spoken IndE but is almost completely absent from written IndE. As for *itself*, although it is rarer overall, it seems to have found its way into written IndE, which might make it 'a candidate for inclusion in an emerging IndE standard' (Lange 2012: 190). In the following analysis of *only* and *itself* in SAVE2020 and CORINNE, we predicted to find more instances of both focus markers in the CORINNE data than in SAVE2020, and more than in ICE-India's written component.

For the data collection and analysis procedure, corpus lines containing the target items *only* and *itself* were extracted using *AntConc* (Anthony 2022) and manually coded as either a 'focus marker' or not by two of the authors, consulting the extended context when necessary. As already noted in Lange (2012: 186), it can often be difficult to separate the restrictive uses of *only* from the presentational ones in the corpus data, for example due to the tendency of IndE speakers to place *only* in final position. Instances of presentational *only* are easier to identify when the context contains quantification, for example 'we are being charged also that much only' (ICE-IND: S1A-054#137, from Lange 2012: 186). In other contexts, it is not always clear. Thus, following Lange (2012: 187), we adopted a conservative approach and chose not to count ambiguous cases of *only* usage towards the final statistics. All in all, the following metrics were computed for each (sub-)corpus: normalised frequency (pttw), the percentage of all instances of *only* which represent presentational/ focus marker uses (FM/TOTAL), the percentage of all clause-final instances of *only* made up by presentational/focus marker uses (FM/FINAL), as well as the percentage of clause-final uses instances of *only* out of all the instances (FINAL/ TOTAL).

Similarly to *only*, it can also be challenging to distinguish cases of presentational uses of *itself* from emphatic uses. More or less clear-cut cases involve the occurrence of temporal adverbials before the target item, such as 'around 4 p.m., itself' (as in example 54). Thus, presentational instances of *itself* were also coded conservatively. After coding the corpus lines, the relative frequency of the presentation uses of *itself* with respect to all instances as well as a normalised frequency (pttw) was computed for both corpora, including separately for each CORINNE sub-corpus. What follows is a summary of the results in Tables 8 and 9 and a detailed discussion.

Based on normalised (pttw) frequencies, presentational *only* was more than twice as prevalent in the CORINNE data than in SAVE2020 (0.015 pttw vs. 0.006 pttw). The absolute frequencies (42 vs. 2), however, support Lange's previous (2007) finding that despite having established itself in spoken language, *only* as a presentational marker is still virtually absent from written IndE. Nonetheless, the numbers suggest that, in CORINNE's more regional newspapers, presentational uses of the focus marker make up a slightly higher percentage of all the instances of *only* (0.173% vs. 0.068%) as well as a higher percentage of instances of *only* in clause-final position (5.45% vs. 2.53%). These results, however, are not significant ($\chi^2 = 0.644$, df = 1, $p > 0.05$, Cramer's $V = 0.036$).[27]

A closer look at the results for the individual sub-components of CORINNE, however, again reveals a more diverse picture. As far as the normalised

---

[27] For this test and the following test of independence, frequencies of *only* as a focus marker and frequencies of clause-final instances of *only* were compared.

Table 8 Frequencies of focus marker *only* in CORINNE and SAVE2020.

Corpus	CORINNE (all)	SAVE2020
only (TOTAL)	24,254	270
only (final)	770	79
only (focus marker)	42	2
pttw	0.015	0.006
FM/TOTAL	0.173%	0.068%
FM/FINAL	5.45%	2.53%
FINAL/TOTAL	3.17%	2.67%

frequencies are concerned, the COR-C component contains the highest number of presentational *only* (0.096 pttw). Excepting COR-UT-AN, where no instances of the focus marker could be identified, the lowest normalised frequency belongs to the COR-NE sub-corpus, with 0.005 pttw. These results are significant ($\chi^2 = 34.805$, df = 8, $p < 0.001$, Cramer's $V = 0.207$).

As mentioned previously, one of the features of IndE involves the placement of *only* in clause-final position. To quantify this tendency and also to search for potential regional differences in its prevalence, a 'by-product' statistic was calculated with the available data, yielding the percentage of all clause-final uses of *only* from all occurrences of *only* in the data. Already when comparing clause-final and non-clause-final *only* in CORINNE and SAVE2020, the results are highly significant (3.17% vs. 2.67%) ($\chi^2 = 535.86$, df = 1, $p < 0.001$, Cramer's $V = 0.149$). More interesting results emerged when CORINNE's components were inspected individually ($\chi^2 = 837.38$, df = 8, $p < 0.001$, Cramer's $V = 0.186$). Although the percentages range anywhere from 2.15% (COR-S) to 6.35% (COR-C) for the majority of the sub-corpora, the COR-W component is a clear outlier with 24.5% of all instances of *only* being clause-final. Based on the interquartile range of FINAL-*only*/TOTAL-*only* for the CORINNE data (3.83%), however, anything above 5.75% can be considered an outlier value, which means that COR-C and COR-UT-AN also count as such.

Contrary to our initial expectations that CORINNE would contain more presentational uses of *itself* than SAVE2020, based on both relative (21.3% vs. 25.2%) and normalised frequencies (0.12 pttw vs. 0.22 pttw), the focus marker *itself* occurs slightly more often in the latter corpus; see Tables 10 and 11 for an overview. These results, however, are not statistically significant when presentational instances of *itself* are compared with non-presentational ones

Table 9 Frequencies of focus marker *only* in the CORINNE sub-corpora.

Sub-Corpus	C	E	N	NCT	NE	S	UT-AN	UT-JK	W
only (TOTAL)	630	2,365	1,710	605	7,156	7,889	1,172	2,229	498
only (final)	40	59	41	21	192	170	73	52	122
only (FM)	7	10	3	2	3	9	0	5	3
pttw	0.096	0.032	0.02	0.029	0.005	0.012	0	0.031	0.006
FM/TOTAL	1.11%	0.42%	0.18%	0.33%	0.04%	0.11%	0	0.22%	0.6%
FM/FINAL	17.5%	16.95%	7.32%	9.52%	1.56%	5.29%	0	9.62%	2.46%
FINAL/TOTAL	6.35%	2.49%	2.4%	3.47%	2.68%	2.15%	6.23%	2.33%	24.5%

Table 10 Frequencies of focus marker *itself* in CORINNE and SAVE2020.

Corpus	CORINNE (all)	SAVE2020
itself (TOTAL)	1,581	270
itself (focus marker)	337	68
FM/TOTAL	21.3%	25.2%
pttw	0.12	0.22

($\chi^2 = 1.8$, df $= 1$, $p > 0.05$, Cramer's $V = 0.033$), thus no statement can be made regarding an association between the use of *itself* as a focus marker and register and/or publication type.

However, the summary statistic for CORINNE is somewhat misleading as it does not paint the whole picture. A closer look at the results for CORINNE's individual components shows once again how much diversity is actually present among the Englishes spoken across India. The normalised frequencies of *itself* as a focus marker range anywhere from 0.06 pttw (for COR-S and COR-UT-JK) and 0.31 pttw (for COR-C). If we compare the sub-corpora based on which percentage of all instances of *itself* are presentational uses, we get a range with COR-UT-JK again at the lower end with 7.2% and COR-UT-AN at the higher end with 48.9%. These results are significant ($\chi^2 = 99.595$, df $= 8$, $p < 0.001$, Cramer's $V = 0.251$). The COR-UT-AN sub-corpus, which had already stood out due to its high incidence of countable mass nouns previously, surprises us again with its high percentage of presentational *itself* uses. COR-NE has the second-lowest percentage of presentational *itself* out of all the components, with 10.5% of all occurrences of *itself*. This could be due to the distinct and diverse linguistic make-up of the region (consisting predominantly of languages belonging to the Sino-Tibetan, Kra-Dai, and Austro-Asiatic language families) and a less strong influence of Indo-Aryan and Dravidian languages, which are theorised to have been the source behind the emergence of both *only* and *itself* as focus markers (see Sharma 2003; Lange 2007). COR-S, COR-W, and COR-N are comparable to each other when it comes to the relative frequencies, which is also more similar to the relative frequency of presentational *itself* found in SAVE2020 than in CORINNE's average statistic.

Lange's previous (2007) findings were that *itself* as a focus marker has found its way into the written language whereas the focus marker *only*, while quite common in spoken IndE, is virtually absent from writing. The results of the present analysis appear to confirm this: more instances of presentational *itself*

Table 11 Frequencies of focus marker *itself* in the CORINNE sub-corpora.

Sub-Corpus	C	E	N	NCT	NE	S	UT-AN	UT-JK	W
itself (TOTAL)	50	82	113	34	382	487	45	138	250
itself (FM)	23	28	25	13	40	122	22	10	54
FM/TOTAL	46%	34.1%	22.1%	38.2%	10.5%	25.1%	48.9%	7.2%	21.6%
pttw	0.31	0.17	0.09	0.19	0.14	0.06	0.12	0.06	0.17

were found in the investigated (sub-)corpora than of presentational *only*. As predicted at the outset, more instances of presentational *only* were found in CORINNE than in SAVE2020; this could be due to CORINNE's more regional nature. The focus marker *itself*, however, turned out to be more frequent in SAVE2020. This was reflected in the normalised frequencies for the particle as well as in the percentage of presentational uses of *itself* out of all the instances. Once again, the actual diversity of the Englishes spoken around India became evident when the regional sub-components of CORINNE were examined separately, with the normalised frequencies and the percentage of the presentational uses varying dramatically between regions.

5.3 Verb + *about*

The innovative (and, in some cases, frequent) usage of verbs with particles in IndE has been noted, among others, by Lowenberg (1986) and Sedlatschek (2009). In addition to analysing creative verb combinations with the particles *up*, *down*, *out*, *away*, and *off*, Sedlatschek (2009) also considers the frequency of verbs combining with particles which would be unexpected in standard varieties of English, such as in the forms *investigate into*, *request for*, *stress on*, and *discuss about*. According to him, such combinations emerge mainly as a result of analogy to well-established forms, such as *discussion about*, and 'are usually employed in an unselfconscious manner as minor variants alongside their standard English "preposition-free" companions' (Sedlatschek 2009: 195). In the following, we focus on the distribution of selected verbs + *about* in CORINNE and SAVE2020 in addition to a discussion of creative, previously un- or rarely recorded combinations. Similar to the previous sections, we thus avoid sticking exclusively to what is known in the sense of 'feature lists' that are 'too static to account for what IndE essentially is – . . . variable, innovative at times, and always capable of changing according to the needs of its users' (Sedlatschek 2009: 311).

In order to be able to compare frequencies of verb + *about* and identify the range of combinations in the two corpora, we took three steps: First, we manually looked through all concordance lines with *about* in *AntConc* (Anthony 2022) and noted all possible combinations. Due to the already very large number of tokens yielded this way, we only considered combinations of verb + *about* without any lexical material between the words, such as in *discuss intensively about*. In the next step, we compared the absolute and normalised frequencies of twelve verb + *about* combinations in CORINNE and SAVE2020. Four key aspects influenced the selection for the quantitative analysis: (1) the combination is either a well-known part of IndE (e.g. *discuss about* and *mention about*) or (2) at least one token of the combination could be found in both corpora, (3) the verb + *about* combination would not be considered standard in most varieties, and (4) the identification of relevant tokens needed to remain manageable. The final selection yielded from this analysis, including absolute and normalised frequencies, is provided in Table 12. A more comprehensive overview including additional verbs that did not meet the selection criteria is given in Table A2 in the Appendix. Moreover, we compared the relative frequencies of the five most frequent verb + *about* combinations in CORINNE with the frequencies of these forms in SAVE2020 to get a clearer picture of the preferred variants, namely with or without *about* (e.g. *discuss a topic* vs. *discuss about a topic*). Finally, we also discuss forms that did not end up as part of Table 12 which, however, are either highly frequent in CORINNE or illustrate the productivity of verb + *about*.

The table shows that *discuss about* (55) is the most frequently used form in both corpora, both in absolute and relative terms (9.42 pmw vs. 5.33 pmw). The second most frequently used form, *mention about* (56), occurs at 8.09 pmw in CORINNE and 3.4 pmw in SAVE2020, respectively.

(55) The group generally <u>discussed about</u> their offspring. <SAVE2020– IND_ToI_4641103.txt>

(56) <u>Mentioning about</u> China's economic advancement in the maritime front, ShriSinha emphasized the need to strengthen the A&N Command <COR-UT-AN_AS_City_10.txt>

Forms of *sensitise about* come in third place, with a higher frequency pmw in SAVE2020 than in CORINNE (although the absolute token count is low in SAVE2020 with only seven occurrences). Two combinations, *outrage about* and *recall about*, represent hapax legomena in their corpora. While the tendencies in verb frequencies are similar, the differences between the corpora are statistically significant (χ^2 = 26.168, df = 11, p < 0.01, Cramer's V = 0.199). Fig. 20 shows the mean frequency of the twelve selected verbs + *about* in Table 12 as well as the standard deviation for each corpus.

We can see in the figure that the mean normalised frequency of the twelve selected verbs is higher in CORINNE ($\overline{x}$ = 1.806 pmw, σ = 3.156) than in SAVE2020 ($\overline{x}$ = 1.253 pmw, σ = 1.548). However, several combinations, such as *outrage about*, are rare even in CORINNE. For certain verbs, this can be explained by considering their low frequency even in the more common form without *about*. The verb *elucidate* (an additional example listed in Table A2) and its word-forms, for instance, only occurs forty-three times in all of

Table 12 Absolute and normalised (pmw) frequencies of selected verb + *about* combinations in CORINNE and SAVE2020.

	Verb + *about*	CORINNE abs. freq.	CORINNE freq. pmw	SAVE2020 abs. freq.	SAVE2020 freq. pmw
1	*admit about*	2	0.07	1	0.33
2	*announce about*	9	0.31	2	0.67
3	*comment about*	25	0.88	3	1
4	*crib about*	10	0.35	1	0.33
5	*debate about*	4	0.14	1	0.33
6	*discuss about*	268	9.42	16	5.33
7	*intimate about*	13	0.46	1	0.33
8	*mention about*	230	8.09	12	3.4
9	*outrage about*	1	0.04	1	0.33
10	*recall about*	1	0.04	1	0.33
11	*remark about*	2	0.07	1	0.33
12	*sensitise about*	51	1.8	7	2.33

CORINNE and once in SAVE2020. In other cases, such as *shillyshally about* in CORINNE, the form with *about* is the only token in the entire corpus.

The high standard deviation for CORINNE can be explained by the largest outliers in the dataset (most significantly *discuss about* with 9.42 pmw in CORINNE vs. 5.33 pmw in SAVE2020), which is why considering additional measures of dispersion that are less susceptible to outliers may be useful. The mean absolute deviation (MAD) is 2.32 for CORINNE and 1.22 for SAVE2020 and thus confirms the relation suggested by the standard deviation (CORINNE > SAVE2020): a lower MAD value means that the distances between the individual frequencies and the mean is lower in SAVE2020 than in CORINNE. The interquartile range (i.e. the range of the middle 50%

Mean Frequency and Standard Deviation of verb + *about*

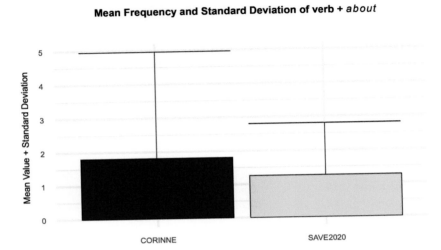

Figure 20 Mean normalised frequency and standard deviation of verb + *about* combinations in CORINNE and SAVE2020.

of all values) is 1.5 for CORINNE and 1.67 for SAVE2020, which shows that the middle portion of the data in SAVE2020 spreads out slightly more than in CORINNE.

Finding out to what extent the verb + *about* variants are preferred over their counterparts without *about* is possible by comparing their relative frequencies. Thus, we compare the absolute and relative frequencies for the five most frequent verb + *about* combinations in CORINNE with the frequencies found in SAVE2020 in Table 13.

The distribution of the relative frequencies in Table 13 confirms that, while verb + *about* 'combinations are indeed recurrent in contemporary IndE, but . . . not generally preferred' (Sedlatschek 2009: 167), there are, again, differences between the corpora. Interestingly, the highest frequency of the verb + *about* combination occurs with *sensitise* in both corpora; the percentage of 75.86% for SAVE2020 is the highest of all verbs in the table. However, thirty of the fifty-one tokens (or 58.82%) in CORINNE occur in the sub-corpus for COR-UT-AN and, for SAVE2020, the absolute frequencies are quite low. No instances of *highlight about* could be found in SAVE2020, which suggests that the form is still limited to less acrolectal newspaper language. For *discuss/discuss about*, *mention/mention about*, and *comment/comment about*, the distributions are similar in both corpora, although the variant without *about* is higher in

Table 13 Absolute and relative frequencies for the five most frequent verb + *about* combinations in CORINNE compared with SAVE2020.

	CORINNE absolute freq.	CORINNE relative freq.	SAVE2020 absolute freq.	SAVE2020 relative freq.
discuss / discuss about	5,030 / 268	94.67% / 5.33%	442 / 16	96.51% / 3.49%
mention / mention about	5,081 / 230	95.67% / 4.33%	420 / 12	97.22% / 2.78%
highlight / highlight about	3,369 / 108	96.89% / 3.11%	214 / 0	100% / 0%
sensitise / sensitise about	677 / 51	92.99% / 7.01%	22 / 7	75.86% / 24.14%
comment / comment about	1,149 / 25	97.87% / 2.13%	152 / 3	98.06% / 1.94%

SAVE2020 for all cases, again suggesting a slightly higher degree of openness to creative, possibly nativising forms in CORINNE.

Sedlatschek (2009: 168), who counted the frequencies of *discuss* versus *discuss about* in ICE-India, found that 88.57% ($n = 31$) tokens occur without and 11.43% ($n = 4$) tokens occur with *about* in the written portion of the corpus. Thus, the relative frequency of *discuss about* is somewhat higher in written ICE-India compared to both CORINNE and SAVE2020. However, these results are strongly mitigated by the fact that ICE is much smaller and contains text types that are more open to innovation than either regional or supra-regional newspapers.

In terms of verbs that may or even tend to occur with *about* (compared to other verbs), examples such as (57) and (58) illustrate that almost all identified combinations are used following what Hartford (1989: 103) calls 'Disquisition verbs' (or 'verbs of saying').

(57) The police had to later clarify about the incident <COR-UT-JK _KO_Indepth_03.txt>

(58) the Indira Gandhi National Open University offers Certificate in Teaching of Primary School Mathematics (CTPM) of 6-months duration. It aims to refresh about children's learning processes in the context of mathematics learning. <COR-UT-AN_AS_City_01.txt>

Using a cognitive-linguistic framework, Hartford (1989: 113) suggests for Nepali English that, at least in the early stages of the variety's emergence, prototype effects played a major role in the acquisition of verb + *about* and comparable constructions. For new learners of the variety, these same prototype effects may still be a factor, but, at some point, the construction has become readily available to language users and has, essentially, become nativised. This is when analogy starts to play a bigger role, since creative expansion can occur based on forms that are already stable parts of the variety.

Overall, this section has shown that verb combinations with *about* occur more frequently in CORINNE than in SAVE2020. Due to their limited regional scope and potentially less rigid editing practices, creative usages have a higher chance of 'surviving' in the newspapers featured in CORINNE. However, despite the significant differences in terms of frequency, the form with *about* does not represent a majority option in any case. On the contrary, for most verbs, the relative frequency of verb + *about* is well below 10% (except for *sensitise about* in SAVE2020). Thus, observing potential frequency shifts in the future is the only way of finding out if verb + *about* ever becomes a preferred option over the alternative without *about*, although these forms are already far from atypical in IndE at either the regional or supra-regional level.

5.4 'Intrusive *As*'

Another fascinating development has been noticed in the 'intrusive *as*'-construction in South Asian and, specifically, IndEs (see line 3 in Fig. 21). Both Koch et al. (2016) and Lange (2016) found an increase in the frequency and creative uses, that is, the different forms or 'types', of this construction. 'Intrusive *as*' occurs in complex-transitive complementation with verbs that have a naming or labelling function, illustrated by sentences such as *I term her as a linguist*: The verb *term* takes both a direct object and an object complement; the object complement is overtly marked with *as*. 'Intrusive *as*' is rare in BrE, namely the historical input variety of IndE, but has already been noted as a feature of IndE in the 1970s by Nihalani et al. (1979). We consider 'intrusive *as*' a good example feature in a comparison of CORINNE and SAVE2020, since, based on the type of language deliberately included in the two corpora, a higher token frequency might be expected in CORINNE. However, Koch et al. (2016) identified a noticeable proportion of 'intrusive *as*' for the verbs CALL, DECLARE, DEEM, DUB, NAME, and TERM in SAVE2011, suggesting that the feature is not restricted to spoken or spoken-like language. Instead, their findings indicate that the feature is on the rise even in educated, written IndE. This has clearly opened the door for the feature to spread even further, which

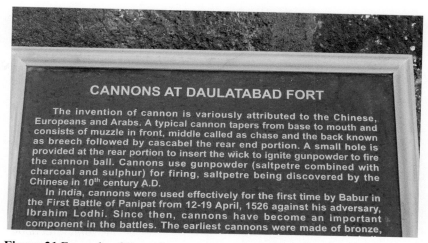

Figure 21 Example of 'intrusive *as*' (picture taken by Claudia Lange in Daulatabad Fort, Maharashtra, in 2016).

makes a comparison of less and more acrolectal (and more or less rigidly edited) language highly interesting.

For the quantitative portion of this case study, we extracted all word-forms of three verbs with and without 'intrusive *as*' using *AntConc* (Anthony 2022): TERM, DEEM, and DUB. We decided on these verbs because they are known to occur with 'intrusive *as*' at least to some extent (see Koch et al. 2016) and represent, relative to each other, instances of high-frequency (TERM), medium-frequency (DEEM), and low-frequency (DUB) verbs.[28] We considered all possible word-forms of each lemma, for instance *term*, *terms*, *termed*, and *terming* for TERM. The initial clean-up after searching for the forms in *AntConc* (Anthony 2022) mainly consisted of removing irrelevant hits. The form *terms*, for instance, may represent either the plural of the noun *term* or the third person singular form of the verb, only the latter of which is relevant for the case study. After this first round of cleaning the data, all relevant tokens were then annotated as either 'regular' or 'intrusive *as*' in Microsoft Excel. For the tokens found in CORINNE, we also annotated the region in which the newspaper containing a token is predominantly distributed. The tokens identified this way are the basis for the two following questions that guided our analysis:

---

[28] In the OED, TERM and DEEM are both listed in frequency band 6 (10–99 pmw) and DUB is listed in frequency band 5 (1–9.9 pmw). However, previous studies (e.g. Koch et al. 2016) have found TERM to be highly frequent (and much more frequent than both DEEM and DUB) in IndE newspaper language, which we could confirm with the case study at hand.

(1) Does 'intrusive *as*' occur more frequently with DEEM, DUB, and TERM in CORINNE than in SAVE2020 and are there frequency differences between the verbs?

(2) Are there regional differences in the token distribution in the sub-corpora of CORINNE?

The absolute and relative frequencies of DEEM, DUB, and TERM with and without 'intrusive *as*' are illustrated in Table 14. The figures presented in Table 14 show that, for every verb, 'intrusive *as*' is more frequent in CORINNE than in SAVE2020, although the difference is statistically not significant at $p > 0.05$. However, there are noteworthy differences between the verbs: for *term as*, the difference between the two corpora is much less pronounced than for the other two verbs. This may be due to frequency effects, since a construction that is already used a lot is likely going to be used even more, and *term as* appears to have won out as the overall preferred variant in Indian newspaper English. When comparing the frequencies in CORINNE and SAVE2020 to the findings presented in Koch et al. (2016: 163), we can see that the distribution of roughly 2/3 of tokens without and 1/3 of tokens with 'intrusive *as*' appears to be consistent for TERM (68.61% of tokens occur as *term as* and the remaining 31.39% as *term* in Koch et al. 2016).

A potential argument for the higher frequency of 'intrusive *as*' in certain regional contexts is based on language contact: the presence of a quotative fulfilling a similar function to that of 'intrusive *as*' in one or more of the contact languages of a language user may lead to higher frequencies of 'intrusive *as*' in their language production. While a fine-grained analysis of contact-induced change is beyond the scope of this Element (although considering the grammatical structures of the involved languages closely may be important; see Sharma 2009), taking a bird's-eye perspective is possible. Consider Fig. 22, in which we illustrate the frequency distribution of 'intrusive *as*' in the regions and states covered in CORINNE.

The size and colour of the dots in the map depends on the overall percentage of 'intrusive *as*' with DEEM, DUB, and TERM in the newspaper components of the respective region; thus, the larger the dot and the closer to a yellowish hue, the higher the percentage. In terms of regional distribution, the map shows that, with some exceptions such as Kerala in the South, states located further in the North of India tend to have lower frequencies and states in the South tend to have higher frequencies of 'intrusive *as*'. Overall, these frequencies map onto the presence or absence of a quotative with an 'identifier' function: Such quotatives fulfil the function of naming and labelling and are, therefore, the likeliest candidates for being model constructions for 'intrusive *as*' in language contact.

Table 14 Frequencies of DEEM, DUB, and TERM with and without 'intrusive *as*' in CORINNE and SAVE2020.

	CORINNE	**SAVE2020**
deem vs. *deem as*	*deem*: 198 (80.49%) vs. *deem as*: 48 (**19.51%**)	*deem*: 25 (92.59%) vs. *deem as*: 2 (**7.41%**)
dub vs. *dub as*	*dub*: 52 (25.12%) vs. *dub as*: 155 (**74.88%**)	*dub*: 15 (48.39%) vs. *dub as*: 16 (**51.61%**)
term vs. *term as*	*term*: 580 (31.99%) vs. *term as*: 1233 (**68.01%**)	*term*: 92 (34.07%) vs. *term as*: 178 (**65.93%**)
Total percentage without vs. with 'intrusive *as*'	no *as*: 45.87% vs. 'intrusive *as*': **54.13%**	no *as*: 58.35% vs. 'intrusive *as*': **41.65%**

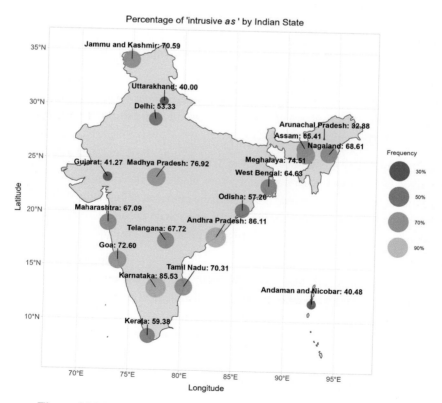

Figure 22 Map of India with percentages of 'intrusive *as*' by state.

For instance, Hindi and Bangla, both Indo-Aryan languages spoken predominantly in the North of India, do not have such an identifier. In contrast, Tamil and Telugu, as major Dravidian languages spoken predominantly in the South of India, do. While there are exceptions (such as Oriya, an Indo-Aryan language with a relevant quotative; see Kachru 1979: 71), there are fewer Indo-Aryan languages with identifier quotatives compared to Dravidian languages, thus lending support to a (soft) contact hypothesis. Again, the situation is obviously more complex: Multilingualism is abundant in India; a writer contributing to a newspaper may not have the regionally dominant language as their L1; individual exposure to the feature may differ; and so on. Nevertheless, contact seems to have some effect, at least, and CORINNE overall appears to 'give way' to these effects to a larger extent than SAVE2020. In addition to language contact, Koch et al. (2016) identified the syntactic distance, in terms of words between verb and object complement, as a significant intra-linguistic factor influencing the absence or presence of 'intrusive *as*'. The long distance between verb and object complement in (59) and the rather extreme example (60) illustrates one of the potential key functions of 'intrusive *as*', the overt marking of object complements in order to create redundancy (Schneider 2012) or, in Rohdenburg's (1996) terms, 'explicitness'. Examples of this type can be found in both CORINNE and SAVE2020.

(59) dubbed the 5.5 km spillway and spill channel being constructed to enable discharge of 50 lakh cusecs of water as the largest in the world <COR-S-Andhra_HI_Andhra_07.txt>

(60) Joint Action Committee (JAC) of Tribal Hohos on Delimitation has termed BJP national general secretary Ram Madhav's statement in the media about his party recommending postponing the proposed delimitation exercise in Nagaland based on the representation of party's State president Temjen Imna Along and chief minister Neiphiu Rio as an insult to the Parliament <COR-NE-Nagaland_NP_State_03.txt>

However, there are also examples such as (61) without any additional linguistic material between verb and object complement apart from the *as* itself; again, both corpora feature such instances.

(61) After years of humiliation, having been falsely dubbed as a spy and sent to jail, former ISRO scientist S Nambi Narayanan is a happy man now. <SAVE2020–IND_TS_4339247.txt>

While we can observe tendencies, usage of 'intrusive *as*' is not consistent across verbs, newspapers, states, or regions of India. Sometimes, the same newspaper, *Kolkata 24x7* in the following examples, features similar constructions both with (62) and without *as* (63).

(62) The Trinamool Congress leadership, however, <u>termed</u> the allegations <u>as</u> baseless and claimed that its party <COR-E-WestBengal_K247_Westbengal_06. txt>

(63) The BJP <u>termed</u> the allegations baseless and said it was goons supported <COR-E-WestBengal_K247_Westbengal_06.txt>

In addition to 'intrusive *as*', other strategies to create redundancy occur as well. For instance, SAVE2020 features example (64) with a token of *was* instead of *as*.

(64) He <u>termed</u> the decision of withdrawal of SAD from the Delhi polls on account of differences with BJP on the CAA <u>was</u> 'unacceptable'. <SAVE2020-IND_TS_4625813.txt>

Finally, exploring the corpora reveals that there are undocumented combinations with 'intrusive *as*' in both corpora; see *vitiate as* in CORINNE (65) and *christen as* in SAVE2020 (66).

(65) The poll atmosphere <u>has been vitiated as</u> communal and divisive agendas are dominating the debate. <COR-S-Telangana_TT_Editorial_02.txt>

(66) <u>Christened as</u> 'Double Smart', the thought of a sequel striked Puri during the scripting stages itself. <SAVE2020–IND_ToI_4510951.txt>

Such examples should make future investigations of 'intrusive *as*' highly interesting, since they might reveal if certain forms have become stable parts of either regional or supra-regional IndEs. However, constructions involving verbs such as *christen* and *vitiate* may also be ephemeral in nature, since they are often low-frequency items that are not used highly frequently with or without 'intrusive *as*'.

In sum, the success story of 'intrusive *as*' is clearly not limited to regional IndEs and, thus, the difference in usage between CORINNE and SAVE2020 is not categorical. 'Intrusive *as*' occurs with various verbs in both CORINNE and SAVE2020 and differences are rather of a quantitative nature, with more tokens occurring in CORINNE for DEEM, DUB, and TERM and, very likely, other verbs. Language contact, in conjunction with analogy and other processes, probably led to the emergence of the feature at some point in the history of IndE, and it continued to spread possibly due to the forms 'establishing a more systematic and transparent form–meaning mapping' (Schneider 2020: 38).

6 Conclusion

In the following, we will first summarise our main results separately for each level of linguistic analysis that we investigated. We will then consider the larger picture that emerges for the unity and diversity of Indian English(es) and for the study of regional differentiation in world Englishes in general.

Towards the end of the last millennium, Strevens (1980: 86–87) and Kachru (passim) employed *Indian English* as a monolithic, homogeneity-implying umbrella term for all varieties of English in South Asia; a conceptualisation which at first met with little resistance until initially anecdotal and later empirical documentations of SAEs outside the borders of India made it obvious that, for instance, Pakistani (Shakir 2020) and Sri Lankan English (Gunesekera 2005; Meyler 2007; Bernaisch 2015) were to be regarded as varieties of English in their own right. Still, the recognition of national varieties of English outside India required academic curiosity to reveal and the compilation and analysis of corpora to empirically document the unique structural profiles of Indian, Pakistani, and Sri Lankan English, while other varieties of English in Bangladesh, the Maldives, and Nepal still largely await such structural descriptions. In this light, it is probably not an exaggeration to consider the recognition of the plurality of SAEs a paradigm shift in the conceptualisation of world Englishes – for which the empirical study of corpus-linguistic resources was a prerequisite. This Element contributes to a novel and timely type of paradigm shift in SAEs specifically, but also in the world Englishes paradigm more generally by challenging the assumed intra-national homogeneity of regional varieties on empirical grounds.

Section 4 investigated structural choices on the word level, namely spelling preferences, register characteristics, and unrecorded lexemes. The orthographic choices under scrutiny were inspired by Pam Peters' *Langscape* project, so that the detailed data in Section 4.1 can be used to align both national and regional IndEs with more general trends in varieties of English world-wide. Similarly, Section 4.3 on hitherto unrecorded lexical items highlights the innovative potential of IndEs for enriching the global English lexicon. Turning now to the intra-varietal perspective, we find that spelling preferences as presented in Section 4.1 profiled a comparatively homogeneous group consisting of COR-E, COR-NE, COR-S, and SAVE2020, suggesting that a potentially increasingly important spelling standard, which, however, is yet to spread across India in its entirety, might have emerged in the North-East, East, and South of India. The most notable deviations from this emerging standard could be observed with COR-C and COR-UT.

These two CORINNE corpus components – and particularly COR-C – also stand out in terms of their register characteristics as shown in Section 4.2. With the exception of Dimension 5: abstract versus non-abstract information, COR-C receives extreme scores often notably removed from or opposed to the other corpus components on each dimension analysed, profiling the texts in COR-C as conceptually comparatively written. In contrast, COR-E and SAVE2020 feature remarkably more speech-like texts while COR-N, COR-NE, COR-S, and COR-UT produce relatively average scores across the MDA scales.

Also with regard to unrecorded lexemes, COR-C is noteworthy in that none of the unrecorded lexemes CRACKERLESS, IMPLEADMENT, SAFFRONISATION, SAFFRONISE, or TELECALLER can be encountered in its texts. Although only SAFFRONISATION, SAFFRONISE, and TELECALLER are attested in it, COR-E features – on average – the highest frequencies of said unrecorded lexemes, whereas each unrecorded vocabulary item is represented in SAVE2020.

Section 5 addressed morphosyntactic choices that have been previously attested for IndE, covering on the one hand features that are commonly attributed to new Englishes generally, such as the blurring of the mass-/count noun distinction (Section 5.1) and new verb + particle combinations with *about* (Section 5.3). On the other hand, the occurrence of *only* and *itself* as presentational focus markers (Section 5.2) is a unique, contact-induced feature of IndE.

Concerning mass and count nouns, we uncovered significantly more instances of the 28 traditionally uncountable nouns under scrutiny in the CORINNE data than in SAVE2020 (0.83 pttw vs. 0.5 pttw). The results for CORINNE's individual components showed a great amount of regional variability, with the COR-UT-AN and COR-W components containing the highest and the lowest normalised frequencies of countable mass nouns, respectively (1.65 pttw and 0.58 pttw). Still, the individual normalised frequencies of CORINNE's components all surpassed the normalised frequency in SAVE2020. The most frequent countable mass nouns across both corpora were *agitation*, *evidence*, *legislation*, *infrastructure*, and *aircraft*. Although very rare, countable uses of such mass nouns as *cash*, *applause*, *violence*, and *slang* could also be attested. That is, the pattern or rule is 'productive' in the sense that new forms are being created beyond the 'usual suspects' included in feature-list approaches to IndE.

Our analysis of *only* and *itself* as presentational focus markers again displayed regional diversity and variability across the individual sub-components, with normalised frequencies of presentational *only* ranging anywhere from 0 pttw to 0.096 pttw. Generally, instances of *only* as a focus marker were slightly higher in CORINNE than in SAVE (0.015 pttw vs. 0.006 pttw), but this result was not statistically significant. The results of this analysis also allowed us to examine the tendency of IndE to place *only* in the clause-final position. It was found that the tendency was most prevalent in the COR-W component, with 24.5% of all instances of *only* being clause-final. The overall low counts of presentational *only* identified in the data appear to confirm Lange's (2007) previous finding that, despite being quite prevalent in spoken IndE, it has not yet found a firm footing in the written language.

More instances of *itself* as a focus marker could be found in the data. However, the results did not conform to our initial expectations that CORINNE would contain more instances thereof. On the contrary, the SAVE2020 data displayed more examples of presentational *itself* (21.3% vs. 25.2% of all uses of *itself*, for CORINNE and SAVE2020, respectively), although here again the difference is not statistically significant. The individual results for the CORINNE components were once again highly diverse, with the percentages of presentational *itself* ranging from 7.2% (for COR-UT-JK) to 47.9% (for COR-UT-AN).

Sections 5.3 and 5.4 were devoted to two verbal constructions which show the surface similarity of an additional particle in IndEs. While particle verbs with *about* are attributed to a wide range of New Englishes, 'intrusive *as*' in complex-transitive constructions has so far only been attested for SAEs. For both features, similar tendencies to those already noted in this Element could be observed: the frequency pmw is consistently higher in CORINNE than in SAVE2020. However, in contrast to verb + *about*, the differences for 'intrusive *as*' are not significant and, for certain variants, such as *term as*, the frequencies are at a comparable level in CORINNE and SAVE2020 (ca. 68% vs. 66%). *Dub as* and *term as* are outstanding in that they represent the majority option across corpora, which means that they have clearly become entrenched even in comparatively formal newspaper registers. Importantly, regional differences need to be emphasised. While certain Indian states strongly favour 'intrusive *as*', it is much less common in others, at least for the verbs DEEM, DUB, and TERM.

The summary of these results leaves us with a complex picture of the unity and diversity of IndEs. Our analyses uncovered shifting degrees of regional differentiation, ranging from marginally to highly different frequencies for individual features under scrutiny. Differences between the national, supra-local level represented by the SAVE2020 data and the regional level captured by the CORINNE data were always apparent, but not consistently statistically significant, and never categorical. There is thus a strong case to be made for the overarching unity of IndEs with respect to the tentative emergence and acceptance of local norms, but without one single regional intra-national epicentre.

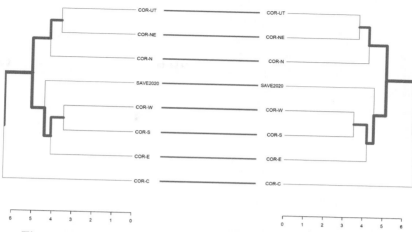

Figure 23 Tanglegram across lexical and lexicogrammatical features.

Sections 4 and 5 provided fine-grained perspectives on how a set of lexical and lexicogrammatical features is distributed across the regional components of CORINNE as well as SAVE2020, but to what extent do these structural preferences reflect a more abstract and generalisable pattern of linguistic unity and diversity within IndE? To get closer to an answer to this question, the insights from the individual analyses for which region-specific data is available were consolidated. We calculated distance matrixes based on Euclidean distance for each of the lexical and lexicogrammatical features' scaled frequencies as reported for the CORINNE components and SAVE2020 in Sections 4 and 5. Subsequently, we amalgamated these feature-specific distance matrixes in one distance matrix and visualised it in the form of the tanglegram in Fig. 23 representing patterns of distance and proximity between the corpus components across the structural features studied. Agglomerative and divisive hierarchical clustering techniques result in the identical cluster structure.

With all due caution in the interpretation at this very abstract level of analysis, the differentiation into three major clusters becomes immediately apparent. COR-Central at the bottom is clearly the outlier, forming a cluster of its own. A regional cluster at the top of the tanglegram comprises the northern, north-eastern, and the Union Territories sub-corpora, the latter also representing data from the northern state Jammu and Kashmir. The central cluster shows that COR-West and COR-South pattern most closely together, then are joined at some distance by COR-East and ultimately also by supra-regional SAVE. This central cluster cuts across the typological division between the Indo-Aryan and Dravidian state languages, covering the regional English newspaper data derived from ten states overall. The sheer extent of this cluster ranging from Tamil Nadu in the South, West Bengal in the East, and Goa in the West of India, and then also including the national level, may be taken to indicate an incipient process of *supralocalisation*, a notion originally suggested for standardisation in the history of English:

> *Supralocalisation* is here used as an umbrella term to refer to the geographical diffusion of linguistic features beyond their region of origin. When supralocalisation takes place, it typically results in dialect levelling, loss of marked and/or rare elements. In this respect it achieves the chief goal of standardisation, to reduce the amount of permissible variation. However, and this should be stressed, many processes of supralocalisation in English, both today and in the past, have been induced naturally by dialect contacts without any conscious effort towards producing an official standard language. (Nevalainen & Tieken-Boon van Ostade 2006: 288)

Again with all due caution, supralocalisation seems to be a fitting notion to capture the clustering of three adjacent regional IndEs plus the national level. However, at this level of abstraction, we cannot 'untangle' the tanglegram; that is, we cannot trace the origin and then the direction of diffusion for the individual features covered in this Element – this has to be left for future research.

From a bird's-eye view, this Element is thus a first attempt to address the overarching question of what empirical picture emerges when researchers refocus their corpus-linguistic attention from international to intra-national perspectives on English in India, contributing to this novel type of paradigm shift in the study of world Englishes discussed at the beginning of this section. Although corpus-linguistic operationalisations of Schneider (2007) pose certain theoretical and methodological challenges (Bernaisch 2015; Hundt 2021; Bernaisch et al. 2022), relevant expectations would be to observe (a) far-reaching structural homogeneity across IndEs, a structural characteristic of endonormatively stabilised varieties as applicable to IndE according to Mukherjee (2007) or Balasubramanian (2009), or (b) orderly internal variability structured around regional and/or social parameters, profiling IndE as a PCE in the phase of differentiation. Still, the question must be permitted whether the diachronic sequencing from homogeneity to ordered internal diversity should be considered the prototypical evolutionary path of PCEs in general and particularly in relation to IndE. It is certainly also conceivable and reconcilable with Schneider (2007) that this diachronic sequencing from homogeneity to ordered internal diversity along regional and/or social lines is predated by a phase of negotiation between competing candidates for a national standard, which, in the aftermath of this negotiation phase, catalyses this transition from homogeneity to ordered heterogeneity envisaged by Schneider (2007).

The empirical findings appear to profile IndE in such a phase of norm negotiation and supralocalisation, combining locally rooted innovative usages on one level of linguistic analysis with adherence to current global trends on another. It is ultimately up to the IndE speech community to negotiate their norms and attribute more or less salience to individual linguistic features so that these become available as markers of social differentiation, indicative of the fifth stage of dialect differentiation in Schneider's (2007) dynamic model. We hope that the rich corpus-based findings of our Element will be taken up both by world Englishes scholars and members of the IndE speech community alike, either for further research on Indian English(es) or for continuing the process of norm negotiation on a firm empirical basis.

Appendix

Table A1 Key indicators for Indian states and union territories.

State	Region	Population[29]	Literacy: overall, men, women	Official[30]/ Main languages[31]	Education: graduates[32]	Children in Std VIII in rural areas who can read simple sentences in English[33]
India		General: 1,210,854,977 Rural: 68.9% Urban: 31.1%	74.04% 82.14%/65.48%	O: Hindi (IA), English	5.64%	45.2%/67.8%

29 Data from the 2011 Census available at https://censusindia.gov.in/pca/default.aspx.

30 Following the Annual Report for 2015 by the Commissioner for Linguistic Minorities in India (http://164.100.166.181/homepage/annualreport.php) for the official language and the main languages of each state in case they are different from the official language(s), and only including main languages with more than 5% of speakers.

31 Abbreviations for language families: IA: Indo-Aryan, DR: Dravidian, TB: Tibeto-Burman, AA: Austro-Asiatic. Census data for population by mother tongue: https://censusindia.gov.in/2011census/C-16.html.

32 Data from the 2011 Census, table 'C-08 Educational level by age and sex for population age 7 and above (total)' (https://censusindia.gov.in).

33 The data come from ASER 2016 (*Annual Status of Education Report*, www.asercentre.org/p/289.html), the last survey to include a test on comprehension of English texts for pupils aged 5 to 16. The Covid pandemic has severely disrupted all education across India, with schools being closed since March 2020. Especially rural areas without the technical and financial means for internet access are heavily affected. The second figure includes 'those who can read sentences, % children who can tell meanings of the sentences'. Gaps in the table indicate insufficient data.

Table A1 (cont.)

State	Region	Population	Literacy: overall, men, women	Official/Main languages	Education: graduates	Children in Std VIII in rural areas who can read simple sentences in English
Andhra Pradesh	**South**	General: 84,580,777 Rural: 66.6% Urban: 33.4%	67.66% 75.56%/59.74%	O: Telugu (DR) Urdu (IA)		71.3%/81.9%
Arunachal Pradesh	**North-East**	General: 1,383,727 Rural: 77.1% Urban: 22.9%	66.95% 73.69%/59.57%	O: English Nissi/Dafla (TB), Adi (TB), Bengali (IA), Nepali (IA)	3.87%	75.9%/93%
Assam	**North-East**	General: 31,205,576 Rural: 85.9% Urban: 14.1%	73.18% 78.81%/67.27%	O: Assamese (IA) Bengali (IA), Bodo (TB)	3.24%	47.8%/59.8%

State	Region	Population	Literacy	Official/Other Languages		
Bihar	East	General: 104,099,452 Rural: 88.7% Urban: 11.3%	63.82% 73.39%/53.33%	O: Hindi (IA) Maithili (IA), Urdu (IA)	2.94%	43.8%/56%
Chattisgarh	Central	General: 25,545,198 Rural: 76.8% Urban: 23.2%	71.04% 81.45%/60.59%	O: Hindi (IA) Gondi (DR), Odiya (IA)	3.99%	36.2%/56.8%
Goa	West	General: 1,458,545 Rural: 37.8% Urban: 62.2%	87.4% 92.81%/81.84%	O: Konkani (IA) Marathi (IA), Hindi, Kannada (DR)	10.06%	-
Gujarat	West	General: 60,439,692 Rural: 57.4% Urban: 42.6%	79.31% 87.23%/ 70.73%	O: Gujarati (IA) Bhili/Bhilodi (IA), Hindi	5.25%	37.6%/66.3%
Haryana	North	General: 25,351,462 Rural: 65.1% Urban: 34.9%	76.64% 85.38%/66.77%	O: Hindi (IA) Punjabi (IA)	7.4%	71.4%/79.7%
Himachal Pradesh	North	General: 6,864,602 Rural: 90% Urban: 10%	83.78% 90.83%/76.6%	O: Hindi (IA)	6.5%	74%/75.2%

Table A1 (cont.)

State	Region	Population	Literacy: overall, men, women	Official/Main languages	Education: graduates	Children in Std VIII in rural areas who can read simple sentences in English
Jammu & Kashmir	**North (UT)**	General: 12,541,302 Rural: 72.6% Urban: 27.4%	68.74% 78.26%/58.01%	O: Urdu (IA) Kashmiri (IA), Hindi, Dogri (IA)	**5.21%**	74.4%[34]/ 64.4%
Jharkhand	East	General: 32,988,134 Rural: 76.0% Urban: 24.0%	67.63% 78.45%/56.21%	O: Hindi (IA) Santhali (AA), Bengali (IA), Urdu (IA)	4.02%	33.5%/55.7%
Karnataka	**South**	General: 61,095,297 Rural: 61.3% Urban: 38.7%	75.6% 82.85%/68.13%	O: Kannada (DR) Urdu (IA), Telugu (DR)	6.62%	49.6%/76.9%

---

[34] The ASER data include Jammu, Kargil, and Leh.

State	Region	Population	Literacy	Official/Other Languages		
Kerala	**South**	General: 33,406,061 Rural: 52.3% Urban: 47.7%	93.91% 96.02%/91.98%	O: Malayalam (DR)	7.58%	79.6%/91.4%
Madhya Pradesh	Central	General: 72,626,809 Rural: 72.4% Urban: 27.6%	70.63% 80.53%/60.02%	O: Hindi (IA) Bhili/Bhilodi (IA), Marathi (IA)	4.44%	26.7%/55.9%
Maharashtra	**West**	General: 112,374,333 Rural: 54.8% Urban: 45.2%	82.91% 88.82%/75.48%	O: Marathi (IA) Hindi, Urdu (IA)	7.69%	45.9%/67.9%
Manipur	North-East	General: 2,855,794 Rural: 70.8% Urban: 29.2%	79.85% 86.49%/73.17%	O: Manipuri (TB) Thado (TB), Tangkul (TB), Kabui (TB)	7.9%	94.1%/88.7%
Meghalaya	**North-East**	General: 2,966,889 Rural: 79.9% Urban: 20.1%	75.48% 77.17%/73.78%	O: English Khasi (AA), Garo (TB), Bengali (IA)	3.05%	87.3%/86.9%
Mizoram	North-East	General: 1,097,206 Rural: 47.9% Urban: 52.1%	91.58% 93.72%/89.4%	O: Mizo (TB), English Hindi, Bengali (IA)	4.52%	82.2%/90.4%

Table A1 (cont.)

State	Region	Population	Literacy: overall, men, women	Official/Main languages	Education: graduates	Children in Std VIII in rural areas who can read simple sentences in English
Nagaland	**North-East**	General: 1,978,502 Rural: 71.1% Urban: 28.9%	80.11% 83.29%/76.69%	O: English Konyak (TB), Ao (TB), Sema (TB), Lotha (TB)	4.53%	92.4%/95%
Odisha (Orissa)	**East**	General: 41,974,218 Rural: 83.3% Urban: 16.7%	73.45% 82.4%/64.36%	O: Oriya (IA)	4.25%	45.4%/65.9%
Punjab	North	General: 27,743,338 Rural: 62.5% Urban: 37.5%	76.68% 81.48%/71.34%	O: Punjabi (IA) Hindi	6.34%	75%/76.3%
Rajasthan	North	General: 68,548,437 Rural: 75.1% Urban: 24.9%	67.06% 80.51%/52.66%	O: Hindi (IA) Bhili (IA)	4.47%	43.3%/58.6%

State	Region	Population	Literacy	Languages		
Sikkim	North-East	General: 610,577 Rural: 74.8% Urban: 25.2%	82.20% 87.29%/76.43%	O: English Nepali (IA), Bhutia (TB), Hindi, Lepcha (TB)	5.35%	-
Tamil Nadu	**South**	General: 72,147,030 Rural: 51.6% Urban: 48.4%	80.33% 86.81%/73.86%	O: Tamil (DR) Telugu (DR)	7.56%	58.9%/79%
Telangana[35]	**South**	-	-	O: Telugu (DR) Urdu (IA)	-	68,1%/88,5%
Tripura	North-East	General: 3,673,917 Rural: 73.8% Urban: 26.2%	87.75% 92.18%/83.15%	O: English, Bengali (IA), Kokborok (TB)	3.75%	50%/-
Uttarakhand	**Central**	General: 10,086,292 Rural: 69.7% Urban: 30.3%	79.63% 88.33%/70.7%	O: Hindi (IA) Urdu (IA), Punjabi (IA)	9.02%	53.5%/73.8%

---

[35] Telangana was formed as a separate state in 2014, after the completion of the 2011 Census.

Table A1 (cont.)

State	Region	Population	Literacy: overall, men, women	Official/Main languages	Education: graduates	Children in Std VIII in rural areas who can read simple sentences in English
Uttar Pradesh	Central	General: 199,812,341 Rural: 77.73% Urban: 22.27%	69.72% 79.24%/59.26%	O: Hindi (IA) Urdu (IA)	4.96%	35.4%/59.3%
West Bengal	East	General: 91,276,115 Rural: 68.1% Urban: 31.9%	77.08% 82.67%/71.16%	O: Bengali (IA) Hindi	5.29%	37.3%/74.3%
Andaman & Nicobar Islands	UT (South)	General: 380,581 Rural: 62.3% Urban: 37.7%	86.27% 90.11%/81.84%	O: Hindi, English Bengali (IA), Tamil (DR), Telugu (DR)	6.34%	-
Chandigarh	UT (North)	General: 1,055,450 Rural: 2.7% Urban: 97.3%	86.43% 90.54%/81.38%	O: English Hindi, Punjabi (IA)	18.42%	-

Dadra & Nagar Haveli	UT (West)	General: 343,709 Rural: 53.3% Urban: 46.7%	77.65% 86.46%/65.93%	O: Hindi, Gujarathi (IA) Bhili/Bhilodi (IA)	5.58%	-
Delhi	UT (North)	General: 16,787,941 Rural: 2.3% Urban: 97.7%	86.34% 91.03%/80.93%	O: Hindi Punjabi (IA), Urdu (IA)	16.43%	-
Lakshadweep	UT (South)	General: 64,473 Rural: 21.9% Urban: 78.1%	92.28% 96.11%/88.25%	O: English Malayalam (DR)	3.57%	-
Puducherry (Pondicherry)	UT (South)	General: 1,247,953 Rural: 31.7% Urban: 68.3%	86.55% 92.12%/81.22%	O: Tamil (DR), Telugu (DR), Malayalam (DR), English	11.38%	-

Table A2 Verbs + *about* in CORINNE, SAVE2011, and SAVE2020.[36]

	Verb+prep.	CORINNE abs. freq.	CORINNE freq. pmw	SAVE2011 abs. freq.	SAVE2011 freq. pmw	SAVE2020 abs. freq.	SAVE2020 freq. pmw
1	add about	6	0.21	0	0	0	0
2	admit about	2	0.07	0	0	1	0.33
3	allege about	7	0.25	0	0	0	0
4	announce about	9	0.31	0	0	2	0.67
5	brainstorm about	1	0.04	0	0	0	0
6	clarify about	8	0.28	0	0	0	0
7	comment about	25	0.88	2	0.65	3	1
8	contemplate about	2	0.07	0	0	0	0
9	crib about	10	0.35	2	0.65	1	0.33

[36] This table also features the frequencies in SAVE2011 for comparison.

10	criticise about	3	0.11	0	0	0	0
11	debate about	4	0.14	0	0	1	0.33
12	disclose about	13	0.46	0	0	0	0
13	discuss about	268	9.42	5	1.63	16	5.33
14	dither about	0	0	1	0.33	0	0
15	dwell about	1	0.04	0	0	0	0
16	elucidate about	2	0.07	0	0	0	0
17	emphasise about	8	0.28	0	0	0	0
18	enlighten about	4	0.14	0	0	0	0
19	exhort about	1	0.04	0	0	0	0
20	forewarn about	2	0.07	0	0	0	0
21	gab about	1	0.04	0	0	0	0
22	harp about	6	0.21	0	0	0	0
23	highlight about	108	3.8	0	0	0	0
24	hint about	5	0.18	1	0.33	0	0
25	illustrate about	2	0.07	0	0	0	0
26	induct about	2	0.07	0	0	0	0
27	intimate about	13	0.46	5	1.63	1	0.33

Table A2 (cont.)

	Verb+prep.	CORINNE abs. freq.	CORINNE freq. pmw	SAVE2011 abs. freq.	SAVE2011 freq. pmw	SAVE2020 abs. freq.	SAVE2020 freq. pmw
28	investigate about	2	0.07	0	0	0	0
29	mention about	230	8.09	5	1.63	12	3.4
30	narrate about	13	0.46	1	0.33	0	0
31	negotiate about	2	0.07	0	0	0	0
32	opine about	1	0.04	0	0	0	0
33	outrage about	1	0.04	0	0	1	0.33
34	publicise about	1	0.04	0	0	0	0
35	quibble about	3	0.11	0	0	1	0.33
36	recall about	1	0.04	0	0	0	0
37	refresh about	1	0.04	0	0	0	0
38	rehearse about	1	0.04	0	0	1	0.33
39	remark about	2	0.07	0	0	0	0
40	reply about	3	0.11	0	0	0	0
41	scream about	2	0.07	0	0	0	0
42	sensitize/-ise about	51	1.8	2	0.65	7	2.33

43	*shillyshally about*	1	0.04	0	0	0	0
44	*showcase about*	3	0.11	0	0	0	0
45	*squabble about*	1	0.04	0	0	0	0

References

Anthony, Laurence (2015). *TagAnt* (Version 1.2) [Computer Software]. Tokyo: Waseda University. Available at www.laurenceanthony.net/software.

Anthony, Laurence (2022). *AntConc* (Version 4.1.4) [Computer Software]. Tokyo: Waseda University. Available at www.laurenceanthony.net/software.

Asher, Ronald E. (2008). Language in historical context. In Braj B. Kachru, Yamuna Kachru, and Shikaripur N. Sridhar (eds.), *Language in South Asia*. Cambridge: Cambridge University Press, 31–48. doi: https://doi.org/10.1017/CBO9780511619069.004.

Austin, Granville (2009). Language and the constitution: the half-hearted compromise. In Asha Sarangi (ed.), *Language and Politics in India*. New Delhi: Oxford University Press, 41–92.

Balasubramanian, Chandrika (2009). *Register Variation in Indian English*. Amsterdam: John Benjamins. doi: https://doi.org/10.1075/scl.37.

Bernaisch, Tobias (2015). *The Lexis and Lexicogrammar of Sri Lankan English*. Amsterdam: John Benjamins. doi: https://doi.org/10.1075/veaw.g54.

Bernaisch, Tobias and Claudia Lange (2012). The typology of focus marking in South Asian Englishes. *Indian Linguistics* 73(1–4): 1–18. Available at https://nbn-resolving.org/urn:nbn:de:bsz:14-qucosa-224747.

Bernaisch, Tobias, Stefan Th. Gries, and Joybrato Mukherjee (2014). The dative alternation in South Asian Englishes: modelling predictors and predicting prototypes. *English World-Wide* 35(1): 7–31. doi: https://doi.org/10.1075/eww.35.1.02ber.

Bernaisch, Tobias, Benedikt Heller, and Joybrato Mukherjee (2021). *Manual for the 2020-Update of the South Asian Varieties of English (SAVE2020) Corpus*. Version 1.1. Giessen: Justus Liebig University, Department of English.

Bernaisch, Tobias, Stefan Th. Gries, and Benedikt Heller (2022). Theoretical models and statistical modelling of linguistic epicentres. *World Englishes* 41(3): 333–46. doi: https://doi.org/10.1111/weng.12580.

Bernaisch, Tobias, Christopher Koch, Joybrato Mukherjee, and Marco Schilk (2011). *Manual for the South Asian Varieties of English (SAVE) Corpus*. Giessen: Justus Liebig University, Department of English.

Bhatia, Aditi (2020). The 'saffronisation' of India and contemporary political ideology. *World Englishes* 39(4): 568–80. doi: https://doi.org/10.1111/weng.12494.

Bhatt, Rakesh M. (2000). Optimal expressions in Indian English. *English Language and Linguistics* 4(1): 69–95. doi: https://doi.org/10.1017/S1360674300000149.

Bhatt, Rakesh M. (2004). Indian English: syntax. In Bernd Kortmann, Kate Burridge, Rajend Mesthrie, Edgar W. Schneider, and Clive Upton (eds.), *A Handbook of Varieties of English. Volume 2: Morphology and Syntax*. Berlin: Mouton de Gruyter, 1017–130. doi: https://doi.org/10.1515 /9783110197181-133.

Biber, Douglas (1988). *Variation across Speech and Writing*. Cambridge: Cambridge University Press. doi: https://doi.org/10.1017/CBO9780511621024.

Biber, Douglas (1989). A typology of English texts. *Linguistics* 27: 3–43. doi: https://doi.org/10.1515/ling.1989.27.1.3.

Biber, Douglas and Susan Conrad (2019). *Register, Genre, and Style*. Second edition. Cambridge: Cambridge University Press. doi: https://doi.org/10 .1017/9781108686136.

Carls, Uwe (2017). *A Dictionary of Indian English with a Supplement on Word-Formation Patterns* (Peter Lucko, Lothar Peter and Frank Polzenhagen (eds.)). Leipzig: Leipziger Universitätsverlag.

Dalrymple, William (2019). *The Anarchy: The East India Company, Corporate Violence, and the Pillage of an Empire*. London: Bloomsbury Publishing.

Davies, Mark (2016–). Corpus of *News on the Web* (NOW). Available at www .english-corpora.org/now/.

Degenhardt, Julia and Tobias Bernaisch (2022). Apologies in South Asian varieties of English: a corpus-based study on Indian and Sri Lankan English. *Corpus Pragmatics* 6(3): 201–23. doi: https://doi.org/10.1007 /s41701-022-00117-8.

Deshpande, Satish (2018). Caste quotas and formal inclusion in Indian higher education. In Krishna Kumar (ed.), *Routledge Handbook of Education in India*. London: Routledge, 228–49.

Doibale, Kranti, Sachin Labade, and Claudia Lange (forthc.). Indian English usage in the 21st century: enduring colonial norms and emerging local standards. In Nuria Yáñez-Bouza, María E. Rodríguez-Gil, and Javier Pérez-Guerra (eds.), *New Horizons in Prescriptivism Research*. Bristol: Multilingual Matters.

Fisher, Ronald A. (1922). On the interpretation of χ^2 from contingency tables, and the calculation of P. *Journal of the Royal Statistical Society* 85(1): 87–94. doi: https://doi.org/10.2307/2340521.

Funke, Nina (2022). Pragmatic nativisation of thanking in South Asian Englishes. *World Englishes* 41(2): 136–50. doi: https://doi.org/10.1111/weng.12517.

Galili, Tal (2015). dendextend: an R package for visualizing, adjusting, and comparing trees of hierarchical clustering. *Bioinformatics* 31(22): 3718–20. doi: https://doi.org/10.1093/bioinformatics/btv428.

Götz, Sandra (2022). Epicentral influences of Indian English on Nepali English. *World Englishes* 41(3): 347–60. doi: https://doi.org/10.1111/weng.12582.

Graddol, David (2010). *English Next India: The Future of English in India.* London: British Council. Available at www.teachingenglish.org.uk/article/english-next-india.

Greenbaum, Sidney and Gerald Nelson (1996). The International Corpus of English (ICE) project. *World Englishes* 15(1): 3–15. doi: https://doi.org/10.1111/j.1467-971X.1996.tb00088.x.

Gries, Stefan Th. (2018). On over- and underuse in learner corpus research and multifactoriality in corpus linguistics more generally. *Journal of Second Language Studies* 1(2): 276–308. doi: https://doi.org/10.1075/jsls.00005.gri.

Gunesekera, Manique (2005). *The Postcolonial Identity of Sri Lankan English.* Colombo: Katha Publishers.

Hall, Christopher J., Daniel Schmidtke, and Jamie Vickers (2013). Countability in world Englishes. *World Englishes* 32(1): 1–22. doi: https://doi.org/10.1111/weng.12001.

Hartford, Beverly S. (1989). Prototype effects in non-native English: object-coding in verbs of saying. *World Englishes* 8(2): 97–117. doi: https://doi.org/10.1111/j.1467-971X.1989.tb00647.x.

Hock, Hans Henrich (2022). Language contact in South Asia. In Anna Maria Escobar and Salikoko Mufwene (eds.), *The Cambridge Handbook of Language Contact: Volume 1: Population Movement and Language Change.* Cambridge: Cambridge University Press, 299–324. doi: https://doi.org/10.1017/CBO9780511619069.014.

Hundt, Marianne (2015). World Englishes. In Douglas Biber and Randi Reppen (eds.), *The Cambridge Handbook of English Corpus Linguistics.* Cambridge: Cambridge University Press, 381–400. doi: https://doi.org/10.1017/CBO9781139764377.022.

Hundt, Marianne (2021). On models and modelling. *World Englishes* 40(3): 298–317. doi: https://doi.org/10.1111/weng.12467.

Kachru, Braj B. (1994). English in South Asia. In Robert Burchfield (ed.), *The Cambridge History of the English Language. Vol. 5. English in Britain and Overseas: Origins and Developments.* Cambridge: Cambridge University Press, 497–553. doi: https://doi.org/10.1515/9783110819502-033.

Kachru, Braj B. (1998). English is an Asian language. *Links & Letters* 5: 89–108.

Kachru, Braj B. (2005). *Asian Englishes: Beyond the Canon.* Hong Kong: Hong Kong University Press.

Kachru, Braj B. (2008). Introduction: languages, contexts, and constructs. In Braj B. Kachru, Yamuna Kachru, and Shikaripur N. Sridhar (eds.), *Language in South Asia*. Cambridge: Cambridge University Press, 1–28. doi: https://doi .org/10.1017/CBO9780511619069.003.

Kachru, Yamuna (1979). The quotative in South Asian languages. *South Asian Languages Analysis* 1: 63–77.

Koch, Christopher, Claudia Lange, and Sven Leuckert (2016). 'This hair-style called as "duck tail"' – the 'intrusive *as*'-construction in South Asian varieties of English and Learner Englishes. *International Journal of Learner Corpus Research* 2(2): 151–76. doi: https://doi.org/10.1075/ijlcr.2.2.02koc.

Kopf, David (1969). *British Orientalism and the Bengal Renaissance: The Dynamics of Indian Modernization, 1773–1835*. Berkeley: University of California Press.

Kortmann, Bernd, Kerstin Lunkenheimer, and Katharina Ehret (eds.) (2020). *The Electronic World Atlas of Varieties of English*. Zenodo. http://ewave-atlas.org. doi: https://doi.org/10.5281/zenodo.3712132.

Lange, Claudia (2007). Focus marking in Indian English. *English World-Wide* 28(1): 89–118. doi: https://doi./10.1075/eww.28.1.05lan.

Lange, Claudia (2010). 'Hindi never, English ever': language nationalism and linguistic conflicts in modern India. In Ursula Schaefer, Claudia Lange, and Göran Wolf (eds.), *Linguistics, Ideology and the Discourse of Linguistic Nationalism*. Frankfurt am Main: Peter Lang, 133–54.

Lange, Claudia (2012). *The Syntax of Spoken Indian English*. Amsterdam: John Benjamins. doi: https://doi.org/10.1075/veaw.g45.

Lange, Claudia (2016). The 'intrusive *as*'-construction in South Asian varieties of English. *World Englishes* 35(1): 133–46. doi: https://doi.org/10.1111 /weng.12173.

Lange, Claudia (2020). English in South Asia. In Daniel Schreier, Edgar W. Schneider, and Marianne Hundt (eds.), *The Cambridge Handbook of World Englishes*. Cambridge: Cambridge University Press, 236–62. doi: https://doi.org/10.1017/9781108349406.011.

Lange, Claudia and Sven Leuckert (2020). *Corpus Linguistics for World Englishes: A Guide for Research*. London: Routledge.

Leuckert, Sven (2019). *Topicalization in Asian Englishes: Forms, Functions, and Frequencies of a Fronting Construction*. London: Routledge.

Levshina, Natalia (2015). *How to Do Linguistics with R: Data Exploration and Statistical Analysis*. Amsterdam: John Benjamins. doi: https://doi.org/10 .1075/z.195.

Lowenberg, Peter H. (1986). Non-native varieties of English: nativization, norms, and implications. *Studies in Second Language Acquisition* 8(1): 1–18. doi: https://doi.org/10.1017/S0272263100005805.

Maechler, Martin, Peter Rousseeuw, Anja Struyf, Mia Hubert, and Kurt Hornik (2019). *cluster: Cluster Analysis Basics and Extensions*. R package version 2.1.0.

Marshall, P. J. (1988). *Bengal: The British Bridgehead: Eastern India 1740–1828*. Cambridge: Cambridge University Press. doi: https://doi.org/10.1017/CHOL9780521253307.

Masica, Colin P. (1993). *The Indo-Aryan Languages*. Cambridge: Cambridge University Press.

Maxwell, Olga, Chloé Diskin-Holdaway, and Debbie Loakes (2021). Attitudes towards Indian English among young urban professionals in Hyderabad, India. *World Englishes* 42(2): 272–91. doi: https://doi.org/10.1111/weng.12550.

McArthur, Tom (2002). *The Oxford Guide to World English*. Oxford: Oxford University Press.

Mesthrie, Rajend (1992). *English in Language Shift: The History, Structure and Sociolinguistics of South African Indian English*. Cambridge: Cambridge University Press. doi: https://doi.org/10.1017/CBO9780511597893.

Mesthrie, Rajend and Rakesh M. Bhatt (2008). *World Englishes: The Study of New Linguistic Varieties*. Cambridge: Cambridge University Press. doi: https://doi.org/10.1017/CBO9780511791321.

Meyler, Michael (2007). *A Dictionary of Sri Lankan English*. Colombo: Mirisgala.

Mohanty, Ajit K. (2017). Multilingualism, education, English and development: whose development? In Hywel Coleman (ed.), *Multilingualisms and Development: Selected Proceedings of the 11th Language & Development Conference, New Delhi, India 2015*. London: British Council, 261–80. Available at www.teachingenglish.org.uk/article/multilingualisms-and-development.

Mohanty, Ajit K. (2019). Language policy in education in India. In Andy Kirkpatrick and Anthony J. Liddicoat (eds.), *The Routledge International Handbook of Language Education Policy in Asia*. London: Routledge, 329–40.

Mukherjee, Joybrato (2007). Steady states in the evolution of New Englishes: present-day Indian English as an equilibrium. *Journal of English Linguistics* 35(2): 157–87. doi: https://doi.org/10.1177/0075424207301888.

Mukherjee, Joybrato and Tobias Bernaisch (2020). The development of the English language in India. In Andy Kirkpatrick (ed.), *The Routledge Handbook of World Englishes*. London: Routledge, 165–77.

Nevalainen, Terttu and Ingrid Tieken-Boon van Ostade (2006). Standardisation. In Richard M. Hogg and David Denison (eds.), *A History of the English Language*. Cambridge: Cambridge University Press, 271–310.

Nihalani, Paroo, R. K. Tongue, and Priya Hosali (1979). *Indian and British English: A Handbook of Usage and Pronunciation*. New Delhi: Oxford University Press.

Nihalani, Paroo, R. K. Tongue, Priya Hosali, and Jonathan Crowther (2004). *Indian and British English: A Handbook of Usage and Pronunciation*. Second edition. Oxford: Oxford University Press.

Nini, Andrea (2019). The Multi-Dimensional Analysis tagger. In Tony Berber Sardinha and Marcia Veirano Pinto (eds.), *Multi-Dimensional Analysis: Research Methods and Current Issues*. London: Bloomsbury Academic, 67–94. doi: https://doi.org/10.5040/9781350023857.0012.

OED Online (2022). Oxford: Oxford University Press. Available at www.oed.com/.

Pearson, Karl (1900). X. On the criterion that a given system of deviations from the probable in the case of a correlated system of variables is such that it can be reasonably supposed to have arisen from random sampling. *Philosophical Magazine* 50(5): 157–75. doi: https://doi.org/10.1080/14786440009463897.

Peters, Pam (2000). Orthography and identity: an overview of the aims and findings of the *Langscape* project. *English Today* 16(3): 37–41. doi: https://doi.org/10.1017/S0266078400011779.

Peters, Pam (2001). Usage 1: *Kaleidoscope*: A final report on the worldwide *Langscape* project. *English Today* 17(1): 9–20. doi: https://doi.org/10.1017/S026607840100102X.

Peters, Pam (2004). *The Cambridge Guide to English Usage*. Cambridge: Cambridge University Press. doi: https://doi.org/10.1017/CBO9780511487040.

Peters, Pam and Tobias Bernaisch (2022). The current state of research into linguistic epicentres. *World Englishes* 41(3): 320–32. doi: https://doi.org/10.1017/CBO9780511487040.

Plag, Ingo (2003). *Word-Formation in English*. Cambridge: Cambridge University Press. doi: https://doi.org/10.1017/CBO9780511841323.

R Core Team (2022). *R: A Language and Environment for Statistical Computing*. R Foundation for Statistical Computing, Vienna, Austria. Available at www.R-project.org/.

Rohdenburg, Günter (1996). Cognitive complexity and increased grammatical explicitness in English. *Cognitive Linguistics* 7(2): 149–82. doi: https://doi.org/10.1515/cogl.1996.7.2.149.

Satyanath, Shobha (2015). Language variation and change: the Indian experience. In Dick Smakman and Patrick Heinrich (eds.), *Globalising Sociolinguistics: Challenging and Expanding Theory*. London: Routledge, 107–22.

Schilk, Marco (2011). *Structural Nativization in Indian English Lexicogrammar*. Amsterdam: John Benjamins. doi: https://doi.org/10.1075/scl.46.

Schmidtke, Daniel and Victor Kuperman (2017). Mass counts in World Englishes: a corpus linguistic study of noun countability in non-native varieties of English. *Corpus Linguistics and Linguistic Theory* 13(1): 135–64. doi: https://doi.org/10.1515/cllt-2015-0047.

Schneider, Edgar W. (2007). *Postcolonial English: Varieties around the World*. Cambridge: Cambridge University Press. doi: https://doi.org/10.1017/CBO9780511618901.

Schneider, Edgar W. (2012). Exploring the interface between World Englishes and Second Language Acquisition – and implications for English as a Lingua Franca. *Journal of English as a Lingua Franca* 1(1): 57–91. doi: https://doi.org/10.1515/jelf-2012-0004.

Schneider, Edgar W. (2020). Calling Englishes as complex dynamic systems: diffusion and restructuring. In Anna Mauranen and Svetlana Vetchinnikova (eds.), *Language Change: the Impact of English as a Lingua Franca*. Cambridge: Cambridge University Press, 15–43. doi: https://doi.org/10.1017/9781108675000.004.

Schwartzberg, Joseph E. (2009). Factors in the linguistic reorganisation of Indian States. In Asha Sarangi (ed.), *Language and Politics in India*. New Delhi: Oxford University Press, 139–82.

Sedlatschek, Andreas (2009). *Contemporary Indian English: Variation and Change*. Amsterdam: John Benjamins. doi: https://doi.org/10.1075/veaw.g38.

Sethi, J. (2011). *Standard English and Indian Usage: Vocabulary and Grammar*. New Delhi: PHI Learning.

Shakir, Muhammad (2020). A Corpus Based Comparison of Variation in Online Registers of Pakistani English using MD Analysis. PhD thesis. Münster: University of Münster.

Sharma, Abhimanyu (2022). English as a facilitator of social mobility in India: the instrumentality vs. identity debate in language policy research. *English Today* 38(2): 88–91. doi: https://doi.org/10.1017/S0266078420000164.

Sharma, Devyani (2003). Discourse clitics and constructive morphology in Hindi. In Miriam Butt (ed.), *Nominals: Inside and Out*. Stanford: CSLI Publications, 59–84.

Sharma, Devyani (2009). Typological diversity in New Englishes. *English World-Wide* 30(2): 170–95. doi: https://doi.org/10.1075/eww.30.2.04sha.

Shastri, S. V., C. T. Patilkulkarni, and Geeta S. Shastri (1986). *Manual of Information to Accompany the Kolhapur Corpus of Indian English, for Use with Digital Computers.* Available at https://icame.info/icame_static/man uals/KOLHAPUR/INDEX.HTM.

Sridhar, Shikaripur N. (2020). Indian English. In Kingsley Bolton, Werner Botha, and Andy Kirkpatrick (eds.), *The Handbook of Asian Englishes.* Hoboken, NJ: Wiley-Blackwell, 243–77. doi: https://doi.org/10 .1002/9781118791882.ch10.

Strevens, Peter (1980). *Teaching English as an International Language: from Practice to Principle.* Oxford: Pergamon Press.

Suárez-Gómez, Cristina and Elena Seoane (2021). The role of age and gender in grammatical variation in world Englishes. *World Englishes* 42(2): 327–43. doi: https://doi.org/10.1111/weng.12546.

Tallerman, Maggie (2020). *Understanding Syntax.* Fifth edition. London: Routledge.

Tognini-Bonelli, Elena (2001). *Corpus Linguistics at Work.* Amsterdam: John Benjamins. doi: https://doi.org/10.1075/scl.6.

Wiltshire, Caroline R. (2020). *Uniformity and Variability in the Indian English Accent.* Cambridge: Cambridge University Press. doi: https://doi.org/10 .1017/9781108913768.

Yurchenko, Asya, Sven Leuckert, and Claudia Lange (2021a). Comparing written Indian Englishes with the new Corpus of Regional Indian Newspaper Englishes (CORINNE). *ICAME Journal* 45(1): 179–205. doi: https://doi.org/10.2478/icame-2021-0006.

Yurchenko, Asya, Sven Leuckert, and Claudia Lange (2021b). *Manual of the Corpus of Regional Indian Newspaper Englishes (CORINNE).* Technische Universität Dresden, Institut für Anglistik und Amerikanistik.

Cambridge Elements ☰

World Englishes

Edgar W. Schneider
University of Regensburg

Edgar W. Schneider is Professor Emeritus of English Linguistics at the University of Regensburg, Germany. His many books include *Postcolonial English* (Cambridge, 2007), *English around the World, 2e* (Cambridge, 2020) and *The Cambridge Handbook of World Englishes* (Cambridge, 2020).

About the Series
Over the last centuries, the English language has spread all over the globe due to a multitude of factors including colonization and globalization. In investigating these phenomena, the vibrant linguistic sub-discipline of "World Englishes" has grown substantially, developing appropriate theoretical frameworks and considering applied issues. This Elements series will cover all the topics of the discipline in an accessible fashion and will be supplemented by on-line material.

Cambridge Elements ≡

World Englishes

/

Printed in the United States
by Baker & Taylor Publisher Services